PUBLISHER'S NOTE

V&S Publishers has carved a significant niche in the publishing industry over the last decade, having successfully published more than 1000 titles across 9 languages spanning over 50 subject categories. Being known for the quality of content, we have built a reputation of excellence and reliability. We have consistently delivered **"Value & Substance"** to our readers, through a wide range of titles across a variety of genres covering school books, fiction and non-fiction that caters to different people from every section of the society.

The **Olympiad Guidebooks for classes 1-10** across all subjects, launched almost a decade ago, under the **GEN X Imprint**, became a go-to-source for the school students in no time, owing to their invaluable and substantive content written in a guidebook pattern,.

Having successfully sold a million copies of the same and in response to demand by both students as well as shopkeepers nationwide; we now present before you our newly launched **Olympiad Workbook Series**, designed for **classes 1-10 across 4 subjects**.

The workbooks are meticulously curated by a team of experienced educators, researchers and subject matter experts, edited by professionals and peer reviewed by teachers. The team has poured its efforts and expertise into creating a crisp and concise workbook which will help and guide the students to the path of success in Olympiad exams. The **MCQs** identified will not only help in scoring top marks in Olympiads but also inculcate a sense of deeper understanding of the subject, by way of solving **HOTS** and referring to complete solutions at the end of the book.

Here we present our new release– **OLYMPIAD WORKBOOK (NCO) CLASS–9** having following features:

☞ Based on the latest syllabi

☞ MCQs with comprehensive coverage of topics

☞ HOTS Questions liberally included

☞ A dedicated chapter on logical reasoning

☞ Model test paper for thorough practice

☞ Sample OMR sheet for real time simulation

We have made sure through our best efforts, that this workbook strictly follows the latest syllabi and patterns of the Olympiad Examination.

As **V&S Publishers** continuously strive to enhance the readability and maintain the credibility of our academic publications, we seek the support of our valuable readers in influencing and enriching the lives of future generations of students.

P.S. While every care has been taken to ensure the correctness of the content, if you come across any error, howsoever minor, do not hesitate to discuss with teachers while pointing that out to us in no uncertain terms.

We wish you all the best for your exams!

DISTINCTIVE FEATURES

01 — Learning Objectives

They list the whole chapter as subtopics, helping the teachers to guide children in a step-by-step manner.

02 — Multiple Choice Questions

MCQs act as an excellent learning aid, helping you to understand and work on your mistakes.

03 — HOTS (Achievers Section)

The High Order Thinking Questions aim to help the student to solve Application-based questions and gain practical understanding of the subject.

04 — Model Test Paper

Model test paper are provided at the end of each book, which help the student to test the knowledge which they have gained after thorough reading of all chapters.

05 — Answer Key

Detailed Answer Key along with explanations aid the pupil to indentify, understand the mistakes they make during the course of Olympiad preparation.

OLYMPIAD WORKBOOK

NATIONAL CYBER OLYMPIAD

01 Learning Objectives

02 Multiple Choice Questions

03 HOTS (Achievers Section)

04 Model Test Paper

05 Answer Keys and Solutions

06 OMR Answer Sheet

V&S PUBLISHERS

Published by:

V&S PUBLISHERS

F-2/16, Ansari road, Daryaganj, New Delhi-110002
☎ 23240026, 23240027 • *Fax:* 011-23240028
✉ info@vspublishers.com • 🌐 www.vspublishers.com

Online Brandstore: amazon.in/vspublishers

Regional Office : Hyderabad
5-1-707/1, Brij Bhawan (Beside Central Bank of India Lane)
Bank Street, Koti, Hyderabad - 500 095
☎ 040-24737290
✉ vspublishershyd@gmail.com

Follow us on:   

BUY OUR BOOKS FROM: AMAZON FLIPKART

© Copyright: *V&S* PUBLISHERS
ISBN 978-81-978176-6-3
New Edition

DISCLAIMER

CONTENTS

FUNDAMENTALS OF COMPUTER

LEARNING OBJECTIVES

➤ Basic Fundamentals of Computer
➤ Hardware and Software Components
➤ Classification of Computer
➤ Different Computer Generations
➤ Software and related concepts
➤ Types of Languages

MULTIPLE CHOICE QUESTIONS

1. Which device is used to process data?
   (A) CPU
   (B) RAM
   (C) DCU
   (D) VDU

2. Who is known as the father of Computer Science?
   (A) Charles Babbage
   (B) Howard Aiken
   (C) Dr. Herman Hollerith
   (D) Blaise Pascal

3. A computer can be defined as an electronic device that can:
   (A) Carry out arithmetical operation
   (B) Carry out logical function
   (C) Accept and process data using a set of stored instructions
   (D) Present information on a VDU

4. Who designed the first electronics computer – ENIAC?
   (A) Van-Neumann
   (B) Joseph M. Jacquard
   (C) J. Presper Eckert and John W Mauchly
   (D) All of these

5. What are the four key functions of a computer system?
   (A) Input, processing, output, and storage
   (B) Keyboard, display, memory, and disc drive
   (C) Word processing, spreadsheets, database
   (D) Bits, bytes, words, and OSI

6. A Pixel is __________.
   (A) A computer program that draws picture
   (B) A picture stored in secondary memory
   (C) The smallest resolvable part of a picture
   (D) None of these

7. Which device is used as the standard pointing device in computer?
   (A) Keyboard
   (B) Mouse
   (C) Joystick
   (D) Track ball

8. Which number system is usually followed in a typical 32-bit computer?
   (A) Binary
   (B) Decimal
   (C) Hexadecimal
   (D) Octal

9. The earliest calculating devices were
   (A) Abacus
   (B) Clock
   (C) Difference Engine
   (D) None of these

10. Word length of a personal computer is _____.
   (A) 4 bits
   (B) 8 bits
   (C) 16 bits
   (D) 64 bits

11. BIOS stands for
   (A) Basic Input Output System
   (B) Best Input Output System
   (C) Basic Input Output Symbol
   (D) Base Input Output System

12. How are the generations of computers classified?
   (A) By the device used in memory and processor
   (B) By the speed of computer
   (C) By the model of the computer
   (D) By the accuracy of computer

13. What is the capacity of a 120 mm CD?
   (A) 420 MB
   (B) 1000 MB
   (C) 1500 MB
   (D) 700 MB

14. Which of the following holds the ROM, CPU, RAM and expansion cards
   (A) Hard disc
   (B) Floppy disc
   (C) Mother board
   (D) None of these

15. Modem stands for
   (A) A type of secondary memory
   (B) Modulator demodulator
   (C) Mainframe operating device memory
   (D) None of these

16. The Central Processing Unit
   (A) Is operated from the control panel.
   (B) Is controlled by the input which in entered the system.
   (C) Controls the auxiliary storage unit.
   (D) Controls all input, output and processing.

17. The term 'baud' is a measure of the
   (A) Speed at which data travels over the communication line
   (B) Memory capacity
   (C) Instruction execution time
   (D) All of these

18. Which of these is actually a very basic computer?
   (A) Toaster
   (B) Stove
   (C) Calculator
   (D) Light bulb

19. Computer memory that temporarily stores information is called _____.
   (A) CPU
   (B) RAM
   (C) ROM
   (D) IBM

20. The brain of the computer is called the _____.
   (A) CPU
   (B) ROM
   (C) RAM
   (D) IBM

21. A single binary digit is known as _____.
   (A) Bit
   (B) Byte
   (C) KB
   (D) MB

22. The local hard drive is generally the _____.
   (A) A drive
   (B) C drive
   (C) H drive
   (D) S drive

23. The cabinet containing the computer's working parts is known as the _____.
   (A) Workstation
   (B) System unit
   (C) Local hard drive
   (D) None of these

24. The various cards in a PC requires _______ voltage to function.
   (A) AC
   (B) DC
   (C) PC
   (D) None of these

25. What is the name of the printed circuit board?
   (A) RAM
   (B) Mother Board
   (C) ROM
   (D) VRAM

26. Which component of PC maintains data and time
   (A) CMOS RAM
   (B) VRAM
   (C) ROM
   (D) EPROM

27. Data stored in a ROM cannot be changed by the user of a computer?
   (A) TRUE
   (B) FALSE

28. Is the data in a RAM stored on a permanent or temporary basis?
   (A) Temporary
   (B) Permanent
   (C) Both (A) and (B)
   (D) None of these

29. To write, erase, rewrite data on a CD-ROM what type of CD-ROM you should use?
   (A) CD-RW
   (B) CD-R
   (C) DVD
   (D) CD

30. How much data will a high density (HD) DVD hold?
   (A) 1 GB
   (B) 4 GB
   (C) 2 GB
   (D) 4.7 GB

HOTS (ACHIEVERS SECTION)

31. Given below two statements. Which of the following statements is/are correct?
   Statement A: Linux is an example of multitasking operating system.
   Statement B: DOS provides command line interface.
   (A) Statement A is correct
   (B) Statement B is correct
   (C) Statement A and B are correct
   (D) Neither statement A nor statement B is correct
   (E) None of these

32. A computer can be used to support single user and multitasking environment. But a type of computer can used to support multipurpose operating environment on huge volume of information such as for nuclear and plasma physics. Which one of the following types of computers is used for nuclear and plasma physics?
   (A) Mainframe
   (B) Minicomputer
   (C) Microcomputer
   (D) Supercomputer
   (E) None of these

33. Read the following statements:
   Statement 1: A minicomputer has enhanced feature than a microcomputer.
   Statement 2: A supercomputer has enhanced feature than a microcomputer.
   Statement 3: A microcomputer is a small, relatively inexpensive computer with a microprocessor.
   Which one of the following is correct with respect to the above statements?
   (A) Statements 1 is correct
   (B) Statements 2 is correct
   (C) Statements 3 is correct
   (D) All statement are correct
   (E) None of these

34. Alia: In a microcomputer, a central device is called microprocessor which has many functional chips fabricated in it.

Albert: In a supercomputer, parallel processing increases the processing speed of the computer.

John: A small computer that is intermediate between a microcomputer and a mainframe.

Who is correct?

(A) Alia   (B) Albert

(C) John   (D) All are correct

35. Match the following:

1. Microcomputer	A.	Mainframe computer
2. ICL39	B.	1024 bytes
3. Atomic Research	C.	1024 bits
4. Kilobyte	D.	Desktop
	E.	Supercomputer

(A) 1 - D, 2 - A, 3 - E, 4 - B

(B) 1 - D, 2 - C, 3 - E, 4 - A

(C) 1 - B, 2 - C, 3 - D, 4 - E

(D) 1 - A, 2 - D, 3 - B, 4 - E

	A	B	C	D		A	B	C	D		A	B	C	D		A	B	C	D		A	B	C	D
1.	Ⓐ	Ⓑ	Ⓒ	Ⓓ	8.	Ⓐ	Ⓑ	Ⓒ	Ⓓ	15.	Ⓐ	Ⓑ	Ⓒ	Ⓓ	22	Ⓐ	Ⓑ	Ⓒ	Ⓓ	29.	Ⓐ	Ⓑ	Ⓒ	Ⓓ
2.	Ⓐ	Ⓑ	Ⓒ	Ⓓ	9.	Ⓐ	Ⓑ	Ⓒ	Ⓓ	16.	Ⓐ	Ⓑ	Ⓒ	Ⓓ	23.	Ⓐ	Ⓑ	Ⓒ	Ⓓ	30.	Ⓐ	Ⓑ	Ⓒ	Ⓓ
3.	Ⓐ	Ⓑ	Ⓒ	Ⓓ	10.	Ⓐ	Ⓑ	Ⓒ	Ⓓ	17.	Ⓐ	Ⓑ	Ⓒ	Ⓓ	24.	Ⓐ	Ⓑ	Ⓒ	Ⓓ	31.	Ⓐ	Ⓑ	Ⓒ	Ⓓ
4.	Ⓐ	Ⓑ	Ⓒ	Ⓓ	11.	Ⓐ	Ⓑ	Ⓒ	Ⓓ	18.	Ⓐ	Ⓑ	Ⓒ	Ⓓ	25.	Ⓐ	Ⓑ	Ⓒ	Ⓓ	32.	Ⓐ	Ⓑ	Ⓒ	Ⓓ
5.	Ⓐ	Ⓑ	Ⓒ	Ⓓ	12.	Ⓐ	Ⓑ	Ⓒ	Ⓓ	19.	Ⓐ	Ⓑ	Ⓒ	Ⓓ	26.	Ⓐ	Ⓑ	Ⓒ	Ⓓ	33.	Ⓐ	Ⓑ	Ⓒ	Ⓓ
6.	Ⓐ	Ⓑ	Ⓒ	Ⓓ	13.	Ⓐ	Ⓑ	Ⓒ	Ⓓ	20.	Ⓐ	Ⓑ	Ⓒ	Ⓓ	27.	Ⓐ	Ⓑ	Ⓒ	Ⓓ	34.	Ⓐ	Ⓑ	Ⓒ	Ⓓ
7.	Ⓐ	Ⓑ	Ⓒ	Ⓓ	14.	Ⓐ	Ⓑ	Ⓒ	Ⓓ	21.	Ⓐ	Ⓑ	Ⓒ	Ⓓ	28.	Ⓐ	Ⓑ	Ⓒ	Ⓓ	35.	Ⓐ	Ⓑ	Ⓒ	Ⓓ

ALGORITHMS AND FLOWCHARTS

LEARNING OBJECTIVES

- ➤ Concept of Algorithm
- ➤ Flowchart and its symbols
- ➤ Basics of Pseudocode
- ➤ Characteristics of Good computer

MULTIPLE CHOICE QUESTIONS

1. An algorithm is defined as
   - (A) A mathematical formula that solves a problem.
   - (B) A tempo for classical music played in a code.
   - (C) A logical sequence of steps that solve a problem.
   - (D) A tool that designs computer programs and draws the user interface

2. A graphical depiction of the logical steps to carry out a task and how the steps relate to each other is called
   - (A) Flowchart
   - (B) Pseudocode
   - (C) Algorithms
   - (D) Hierarchy chart

3. Which symbol is used to represent output in a flowchart?
   - (A) Square
   - (B) Circle
   - (C) Parallelogram
   - (D) Triangle

4. Which symbol is used to represent terminal symbol in a flowchart?
   - (A) Circle
   - (B) Lozenge
   - (C) Diamond
   - (D) Square

5. If a program will read 100 data records, you read the first data record in a statement that is separate from the other

99. This is called a ________ read.
   - (A) Nested
   - (B) A Stacked
   - (C) Posttest
   - (D) Priming

6. The ________ can be a useful tool when a program needs to be modified months or years after it was originally written.
   - (A) Flowchart
   - (B) Hierarchy chart
   - (C) Pseudocode
   - (D) Variable declaration

7. In a ________ loop, the loop body continues to execute as long as the answer to the controlling question is yes, or true.
   - (A) Do-then
   - (B) Do-when
   - (C) Do-until
   - (D) Do-while

8. A flowchart is an example of tools used in the program ________ phase.
   - (A) Analysis
   - (B) Design
   - (C) Implement
   - (D) Testing

9. The programming tool which uses some symbols to show the sequence of steps needed to solve a programming problem is called __________.
   - (A) Data Flow diagram
   - (B) Flow Chart
   - (C) ER-Diagram
   - (D) Class Diagram

10. An IF-THEN-ELSE statement is part of the _________ structure.
   (A) Selection
   (B) Iteration
   (C) Sequence
   (D) None of these

11. The ______ structure involves repeating a sequence until a condition is met.
   (A) Selection
   (B) Iteration
   (C) Sequence
   (D) None of these

12. Two main measures for the efficiency of an algorithm are ______.
   (A) Processor and memory
   (B) Complexity and capacity
   (C) Time and space
   (D) Data and space

13. The time factor while determining the efficiency of an algorithm is measured by:
   (A) Counting microseconds
   (B) Counting the number of key operations
   (C) Counting the number of statements
   (D) Counting the kilobytes of an algorithm

14. The space factor while determining the efficiency of an algorithm is measured by
   (A) Counting the maximum memory needed by the algorithm
   (B) Counting the minimum memory needed by the algorithm
   (C) Counting the average memory needed by the algorithm
   (D) Counting the maximum disc space needed by the algorithm

15. The worst case occur in a linear search algorithm when
   (A) Item is somewhere in the middle of the array
   (B) Item is not in the array at all
   (C) Item is the last element in the array
   (D) Item is the last element in the array or is not there at all

16. The average case occurs in a linear search algorithm
   (A) When Item is somewhere in the middle of the array
   (B) When Item is not in the array at all
   (C) When Item is the last element in the array
   (D) When Item is the last element in the array or is not there at all

17. The complexity of the average case of an algorithm is
   (A) Much more complicated to analyze than that of the worst case
   (B) Much more simpler to analyze than that of the worst case
   (C) Sometimes more complicated and some times simpler than that of the worst case
   (D) None of the above

18. In which year did John Napier develop logarithm?
   (A) 1416
   (B) 1614
   (C) 1641
   (D) 1804

19. A step by step procedure used to solve a problem is called
   (A) Operating system
   (B) Algorithm
   (C) Application Program
   (D) None of these

20. ______ involves writing instructions and giving them to the computer as input to complete a task.
   (A) Computer Programming
   (B) Computer Program
   (C) Computer Programmer
   (D) None of these

21. A ______ is a set of instructions written in a computer language in order to be executed by a computer to perform a useful task.
   (A) Computer Programming
   (B) Computer Program
   (C) Computer Programmer
   (D) None of these

22. A _______ is a person who translates the task that you want from a computer to do into a form that a computer can understand.
   (A) Computer Programming
   (B) Computer Program
   (C) Computer Programmer
   (D) None of these

23. Which are the characteristics of a good computer program?
   (A) Portability   (B) Readability
   (C) Efficiency   (D) All of these

24. Developing a correct algorithm can be an intellectual challenge while coding is straightforward.
   (A) True   (B) False

25. The most widely used notations for developing algorithms are:
   (A) Flow Chart   (B) Pseudocode
   (C) Both (A) and (B) (D) None of these

26. A ___________ is a diagram containing lines which represent all possible paths through the program.
   (A) Flow Chart   (B) Pseudocode
   (C) Both (A) and (B) (D) None of these

27. Pseudocode is a form of structured natural language.
   (A) Flow Chart   (B) Pseudocode
   (C) Both (A) and (B) (D) None of these

28. Read the following statements and find out if they are true or false:
   1. Pseudocode is an artificial and informal language that helps programmers develop algorithms.
   2. Pseudocode is very similar to everyday English.
   (A) Both are true.
   (B) Statement 1 is true and the other is false.
   (C) Statement 2 is true and the other is false.
   (D) Both are false.

29. Which statement is false?
   (A) A flowchart is a graphical representation of the sequence of operations in an information system or program.
   (B) Flowchart shows logic of an algorithm.
   (C) It helps us to solve any problem easily through pictures than by words.
   (D) None of these

30. Which statement is false?
   (A) An algorithm can be represented diagrammatically in the form of a flow chart.
   (B) A flowchart is basically the plan to be followed when the program is written.
   (C) A flowchart acts like a road map for a programmer and guides him in proceeding from the starting point to the final point while writing a computer program.
   (D) None of these

HOTS (ACHIEVERS SECTION)

31. It is a program planning tool allowing Programmers to plan program logic by writing program instructions in a language, like English, which can be easily converted into real programming statements without using symbols. Identify it.
   (A) Pseudocode
   (B) Flowchart
   (C) High level program
   (D) Assembly language program

32. The symbol displayed in the given flowchart is called a/an ___________.

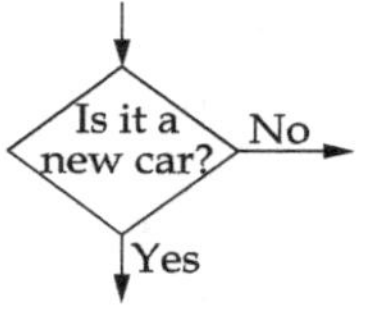

(A) On page connector
(B) Off page connector
(C) Terminal symbol
(D) Decision symbol

33. Which of the following statements hold(s) true about manually drawn flowchart?

   Statement 1: They provide better communication because even the non-programmers can understand the logic of program.

   Statement 2: They can be modified frequently as per the requirement if there is any change.

   (A) Only Statement 1
   (B) Only Statement 2
   (C) Both Statement 1 and Statement 2
   (D) Neither Statement 1 nor Statement 2

34. The arrows displayed here is used for _______ in a flowchart.

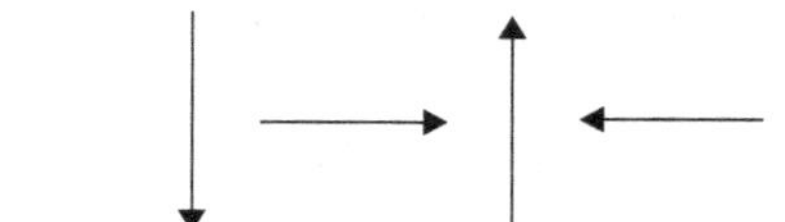

(A) Representing direction and sequence of processes.
(B) Asking questions and then determines which route the program will take
(C) Representing input into the program or output from the program
(D) Representing an action taken by the program.

35. Which of the following statements is INCORRECT in case of a flowchart?

   (A) Program flowcharts serves as a good program documentation and can be used for various purposes.
   (B) Maintaining and operating program becomes easy with a flowchart. It helps the programmer to put efforts more efficiently.
   (C) Any symbol can be used as a part of the flowchart - as desired by the creator of the flowchart.
   (D) Flowcharts acts as a reference during system analysis and program development phase.

Darken Your Choice with HB Pencil

1.	Ⓐ Ⓑ Ⓒ Ⓓ	8.	Ⓐ Ⓑ Ⓒ Ⓓ	15.	Ⓐ Ⓑ Ⓒ Ⓓ	22	Ⓐ Ⓑ Ⓒ Ⓓ	29.	Ⓐ Ⓑ Ⓒ Ⓓ
2.	Ⓐ Ⓑ Ⓒ Ⓓ	9.	Ⓐ Ⓑ Ⓒ Ⓓ	16.	Ⓐ Ⓑ Ⓒ Ⓓ	23.	Ⓐ Ⓑ Ⓒ Ⓓ	30.	Ⓐ Ⓑ Ⓒ Ⓓ
3.	Ⓐ Ⓑ Ⓒ Ⓓ	10.	Ⓐ Ⓑ Ⓒ Ⓓ	17.	Ⓐ Ⓑ Ⓒ Ⓓ	24.	Ⓐ Ⓑ Ⓒ Ⓓ	31.	Ⓐ Ⓑ Ⓒ Ⓓ
4.	Ⓐ Ⓑ Ⓒ Ⓓ	11.	Ⓐ Ⓑ Ⓒ Ⓓ	18.	Ⓐ Ⓑ Ⓒ Ⓓ	25.	Ⓐ Ⓑ Ⓒ Ⓓ	32.	Ⓐ Ⓑ Ⓒ Ⓓ
5.	Ⓐ Ⓑ Ⓒ Ⓓ	12.	Ⓐ Ⓑ Ⓒ Ⓓ	19.	Ⓐ Ⓑ Ⓒ Ⓓ	26.	Ⓐ Ⓑ Ⓒ Ⓓ	33.	Ⓐ Ⓑ Ⓒ Ⓓ
6.	Ⓐ Ⓑ Ⓒ Ⓓ	13.	Ⓐ Ⓑ Ⓒ Ⓓ	20.	Ⓐ Ⓑ Ⓒ Ⓓ	27.	Ⓐ Ⓑ Ⓒ Ⓓ	34.	Ⓐ Ⓑ Ⓒ Ⓓ
7.	Ⓐ Ⓑ Ⓒ Ⓓ	14.	Ⓐ Ⓑ Ⓒ Ⓓ	21.	Ⓐ Ⓑ Ⓒ Ⓓ	28.	Ⓐ Ⓑ Ⓒ Ⓓ	35.	Ⓐ Ⓑ Ⓒ Ⓓ

ANIMATIONS AND MULTIMEDIA

3

LEARNING OBJECTIVES

➤ Concepts related to animation
➤ Concepts related to multimedia

MULTIPLE CHOICE QUESTIONS

1. Green screen video effect is synonyms with ______.
   (A) Morphing
   (B) Chroma key animation
   (C) Stop-motion animation
   (D) Cel-shading

2. The ratio of the ______ in an image is known as Aspect Ratio.
   (A) Horizontal points to product of 'horizontal and vertical' points
   (B) Horizontal to vertical points
   (C) Vertical to sum of 'horizontal and vertical' points
   (D) All of these

3. Stopping an animated character for a specific number of frames is called ___________.
   (A) Freezing
   (B) Slowing
   (C) Pacing
   (D) Panning

4. ______ is a graphics and image handling procedure, in which one image is gradually turned into another.
   (A) Animation
   (B) Morphing
   (C) Multimedia
   (D) Universal

5. In which of the following activities interactive media is applied?
   (A) Chatting
   (B) Watching TV
   (C) Reading newspaper
   (D) All of these

6. Software or hardware filters that adjust the loudness of specific audio frequencies are called ______.
   (A) Equalizers
   (B) Boosters
   (C) Acousters
   (D) Compound meters

7. In computer graphics, ZUI stands for ___________.
   (A) Zoomed Used Internet
   (B) Zoomable User Interface
   (C) Zoomable User Interaction
   (D) Zoomed User Interchange

8. ___________ Category of multimedia progresses without any navigational control.
   (A) Linear
   (B) Non-linear
   (C) Continuous
   (D) Non-continuous

9. In multimedia terminology, _______ is an invisible line, drawn along a character's pose, so that the character's pose will follow along the line.
   - (A) Keyframe
   - (B) Line of flow
   - (C) Line of action
   - (D) Layer

10. Which of the following statements is CORRECT?
    - (A) Random scan monitors draw a picture one line at a time.
    - (B) Raster scan monitors are known as vector displays.
    - (C) Raster scan monitors draw a picture one line at a time.
    - (D) Random scan is better suited for displaying shading and color areas.

11. What do you understand by the term breakdown?
    - (A) A type of animation technique in which a symmetry is defined in a character's pose.
    - (B) A very specific type of in-between that links two keyframes.
    - (C) The last step of animation, where sequence of all the layer is defined.
    - (D) The process of building a template of the character to be animated.

12. Repeating the same action to get a maximum screen time-out of a minimum of moves is called _______.
    - (A) Cut-out animation
    - (B) Track animation
    - (C) Block animation
    - (D) Cycle animation

13. Playing movie through DVD that allows you to go forward and backward is an example of _______ media.
    - (A) Contiguous
    - (B) Non-contiguous
    - (C) Non-Linear
    - (D) Linear

14. The distinction between a graphic and a movie clip is that _______.
    - (A) A graphic is static or stationary whereas a movie is dynamic
    - (B) Movie clip is static or stationary whereas a graphic is dynamic.
    - (C) There is no difference between a graphic and a movie clip
    - (D) None of these

15. Motion graphics _______.
    - (A) Refers to any moving / animated graphics created by use of digital sequencing of frames
    - (B) Is a term interchangeably used with animation
    - (C) Tends to encompass all animated movies
    - (D) All of these

16. Which of the following statements best describes cutout animations?
    - (A) Cutouts are created from existing objects. Then these cutouts are automatically moved.
    - (B) Cutouts are stationary. A moving movie camera is focused on the cut-out and the animated scene is captured.
    - (C) Cutouts are arranged on flat surfaces. They are then moved and repositioned. This way animation is simulated.
    - (D) There exists no animation technique such as cutout animations.

17. The products and services on digital computer based system that uses technology like streaming media and responds to user actions by presenting content in the form of text, animation or images is called _______.
    - (A) Monomedia
    - (B) Footage
    - (C) Rich Media
    - (D) Stagnant Media

18. It is one of the major problem faced by new animators, where they end up making the one half of an animated character's body to move and behave

like its other half, making the character appearance unnatural. What is it called?
(A) Twinning
(B) Morphing
(C) Scaling
(D) Tuning

19. _____ is an anti-aliasing technique. It allows shift of 1/4, 1/2 and 3/4 of a pixel diameter. This enables a closer path of a line.
(A) Pixel phasing
(B) Filtering
(C) Intensity compensation
(D) Sampling technique

20. Identify the following:
It is a technique to create an illusion of animation.
In this a series of picture (gradually different from other) is drawn on every page of a book.
All these pictures appear to animate when pages are turned rapidly.
(A) Motion Book
(B) Roto Book
(C) Flip Book
(D) Random Book

HOTS (ACHIEVERS SECTION)

21. The _____________ is a piece of equipment designed to make cartoons more realistic and enjoyable. It uses stacked panes of glass each with different elements of the animation.
(A) Multiplane camera
(B) VR
(C) Thaumatrope
(D) Phenakistoscope

22. He made the first animated film in 1906.
(A) Walt Disney
(B) J. Stuart Blackton
(C) William Horner
(D) J.A. Ferdinand Plateau

23. Name of the first animation film.
(A) Humorous Phases of Funny Faces
(B) Tom and Jerry
(C) Mickey Mouse
(D) How i learnt animations

24. _____________ animation is used to animate things that are smaller than life size.
(A) Immersive
(B) Claymotion
(C) Stop motion
(D) Augmented

25. The father of animation?
(A) Walt Disney
(B) J. Stuart Blackton
(C) William Horner
(D) J.A. Ferdinand Plateau

—Darken Your Choice with HB Pencil—

1. Ⓐ Ⓑ Ⓒ Ⓓ	6. Ⓐ Ⓑ Ⓒ Ⓓ	11. Ⓐ Ⓑ Ⓒ Ⓓ	16. Ⓐ Ⓑ Ⓒ Ⓓ	21. Ⓐ Ⓑ Ⓒ Ⓓ
2. Ⓐ Ⓑ Ⓒ Ⓓ	7. Ⓐ Ⓑ Ⓒ Ⓓ	12. Ⓐ Ⓑ Ⓒ Ⓓ	17. Ⓐ Ⓑ Ⓒ Ⓓ	22. Ⓐ Ⓑ Ⓒ Ⓓ
3. Ⓐ Ⓑ Ⓒ Ⓓ	8. Ⓐ Ⓑ Ⓒ Ⓓ	13. Ⓐ Ⓑ Ⓒ Ⓓ	18. Ⓐ Ⓑ Ⓒ Ⓓ	23. Ⓐ Ⓑ Ⓒ Ⓓ
4. Ⓐ Ⓑ Ⓒ Ⓓ	9. Ⓐ Ⓑ Ⓒ Ⓓ	14. Ⓐ Ⓑ Ⓒ Ⓓ	19. Ⓐ Ⓑ Ⓒ Ⓓ	24. Ⓐ Ⓑ Ⓒ Ⓓ
5. Ⓐ Ⓑ Ⓒ Ⓓ	10. Ⓐ Ⓑ Ⓒ Ⓓ	15. Ⓐ Ⓑ Ⓒ Ⓓ	20. Ⓐ Ⓑ Ⓒ Ⓓ	25. Ⓐ Ⓑ Ⓒ Ⓓ

FLASH CS6

LEARNING OBJECTIVES

➤ Basics of Flash CS6
➤ Common tools of Flash CS6

MULTIPLE CHOICE QUESTIONS

1. Where is the envelop distort tool located?
   (A) Located at the bottom of the box with a movie clip selected.
   (B) Located at the right of the box with a shape selected
   (C) Located at the bottom of the box with a shape selected
   (D) Located at the left of the box with a shape selected

2. These are used to apply special art effects that give your image the appearance of a sketch or impressionistic painting?
   (A) Tools   (B) Layers Styles
   (C) Blending Mode (D) Filters

3. Items that are stored in the library are considered as?
   (A) Palletes   (B) Symbol
   (C) Library Tools (D) Shapes

4. Which of the following is utilized to store the objects that can be reused throughout the movie?
   (A) Paint Bucket
   (B) Properties Inspector
   (C) Library Panel
   (D) Windows Panel

5. A matrix of frames and layers is called as the?
   (A) Timeline
   (B) Tools
   (C) Scene
   (D) Animations

6. Which of the following will select that which of the timeline is visible on the stage?
   (A) Oval   (B) Pencil
   (C) Pen   (D) Play head

7. The Key frames with the visible content will have?
   (A) Colourful Circles
   (B) Hollow Circles
   (C) Solid Circles
   (D) Blank Circles

8. Typical Frame Rates range from?
   (A) 15 to 30 frames per second
   (B) 15 to 20 frames per second
   (C) 10 to 15 frames per second
   (D) 30 to 45 frames per second

9. How will you make the animation quality better?

(A) Change the orientation

(B) Add a key frame to every frame

(C) Add more animations

(D) Change the colour

10. What do the frames of a button indicate?

(A) The size of the button

(B) Animation which the frame provide

(C) What will be visible when the mouse is over or pressed down

(D) The size of the frame

11. Which of the following statements is NOT true in case of Flash?

(A) Flash files loads faster than animated GIF images.

(B) It is a free software.

(C) It allows interactivity compared to animated images.

(D) It does not require significant programming skills.

12. Which of the following operations can be applied to layers?

(A) You can change the position and order of layers.

(B) You can delete layers.

(C) You can add layers.

(D) All of these

13. Which of the following operations performs the following tasks?

i. Generate the compressed version of your file with swf extension.

ii. Generate an HTML document that activates swf files and specifies browser settings.

(A) Font Mapping   (B) Publish

(C) Snapping   (D) Magnification

14. You can scale, rotate and change the direction of the gradient fill in an object using the _____ tool.

(A) Gradient Transform

(B) Gradient Fill

(C) Polystar

(D) Free Transform

15. Which of the following is NOT a part of the Pen Tool flyout?

(A) Add Anchor Point Tool

(B) Delete Anchor Point Tool

(C) Pin Anchor Point

(D) Convert Anchor Point Tool

16. In _____ layers, you can create strokes that acts as a path for instances, groups or text to be followed.

(A) Guide   (B) Flip

(C) Both (A) and (B) (D) None of these

17. To slow in and slow out the speed of an object in an animation, use ________.

(A) Flipping   (B) Curving

(C) Tweening   (D) Easing

18. The default frame rate in Flash is _____ fps.

(A) 18   (B) 24

(C) 30   (D) 36

19. When you use geometrical primitives such as lines, curves, points and shapes to create graphics, you are using _____ graphics.

(A) Raster

(B) Linear

(C) Vector

(D) Collateral

20. Which of the following is NOT a filter type?

(A) Bevel

(B) Gradient Glow

(C) Gradient Shadow

(D) Gradient Bevel

21. Which of the following is also called as symbol store house?

    (A) Timeline (B) Library
    (C) Stage (D) Scene

22. The _______ symbol is used for animating static images.

    (A) Static
    (B) Instance
    (C) Graphic
    (D) Both (A) and (B)

23. You have created a shape on stage, now you want to add a filter effect to it. How would you do so?

    (A) Convert the shape to Graphic symbol > Select the symbol > Go to Properties tab > Filter > Click on Add filter > Select the desired effect.
    (B) Convert the shape to Movie Clip symbol > Select the symbol > Go to Properties > Filter > Click on Add filter > Select the desired effect
    (C) Convert the shape to Graphic symbol> Select the symbol > Go to Modify tab > Filter > Click on Add filter > Select the desired effect.
    (D) Convert the shape to Movie Clip symbol > Select the symbol > Go to Edit tab > Filter > Click on Add filter > Select the desired effect

24. To maintain a constant orientation of an object with respect to its path, use the _______ check box in the Properties window of Motion Tween.

    (A) Scale
    (B) Snap
    (C) Orient to path
    (D) Sync

25. What would happen when you select a line of text and then go to Modify tab and select "Break Apart" option?

    (A) The text block will get broken into multiple text blocks to edit each character separately.
    (B) The text block will get broken into two parts and each part will get assigned to a separate layer.
    (C) The animation or any effect applied to the text will get removed.
    (D) The text will get copied to all existing layers.

—Darken Your Choice with HB Pencil—

1.	Ⓐ Ⓑ Ⓒ Ⓓ	6.	Ⓐ Ⓑ Ⓒ Ⓓ	11.	Ⓐ Ⓑ Ⓒ Ⓓ	16	Ⓐ Ⓑ Ⓒ Ⓓ	21.	Ⓐ Ⓑ Ⓒ Ⓓ
2.	Ⓐ Ⓑ Ⓒ Ⓓ	7.	Ⓐ Ⓑ Ⓒ Ⓓ	12.	Ⓐ Ⓑ Ⓒ Ⓓ	17.	Ⓐ Ⓑ Ⓒ Ⓓ	22.	Ⓐ Ⓑ Ⓒ Ⓓ
3.	Ⓐ Ⓑ Ⓒ Ⓓ	8.	Ⓐ Ⓑ Ⓒ Ⓓ	13.	Ⓐ Ⓑ Ⓒ Ⓓ	18.	Ⓐ Ⓑ Ⓒ Ⓓ	23.	Ⓐ Ⓑ Ⓒ Ⓓ
4.	Ⓐ Ⓑ Ⓒ Ⓓ	9.	Ⓐ Ⓑ Ⓒ Ⓓ	14.	Ⓐ Ⓑ Ⓒ Ⓓ	19.	Ⓐ Ⓑ Ⓒ Ⓓ	24.	Ⓐ Ⓑ Ⓒ Ⓓ
5.	Ⓐ Ⓑ Ⓒ Ⓓ	10.	Ⓐ Ⓑ Ⓒ Ⓓ	15.	Ⓐ Ⓑ Ⓒ Ⓓ	20.	Ⓐ Ⓑ Ⓒ Ⓓ	25.	Ⓐ Ⓑ Ⓒ Ⓓ

VISUAL BASIC

LEARNING OBJECTIVES

➤ Visual Studio Components
➤ Basic of Visual Basics

MULTIPLE CHOICE QUESTIONS

1. Visual Basic responds to events using which of the following?
   (A) A code procedure
   (B) An event procedure
   (C) A form procedure
   (D) A property

2. When the user clicks a button, _________ is triggered.
   (A) An event
   (B) A method
   (C) A setting
   (D) A property

3. Which property of controls tells the order they receive the focus when the tab key is pressed during run time?
   (A) Focus order
   (B) Focus number
   (C) Tab index
   (D) Control order

4. Sizing handles make it very easy to resize virtually any control while developing applications with Visual Basic. When working in the Form Designer, how are these sizing handles displayed?
   (A) A rectangle with 4 arrows, one in each corner, around your control.
   (B) A 3-D outline around your control.
   (C) A rectangle with small squares around your control.
   (D) None of these.

5. The Properties window plays an important role in the development of Visual Basic applications. It is mainly used
   (A) To change how objects look and feel.
   (B) When opening programs stored on a hard drive.
   (C) To allow the developer to graphically design program components.
   (D) To set program related options like Program Name, Program Location, etc.

6. Which of the properties in a control's list of properties is used to give the control a meaningful name?
   (A) Text
   (B) ContextMenu
   (C) ControlName
   (D) Name

7. Keywords in Visual Basic are words that
   (A) Should be used while naming variables.
   (B) Are used to name controls, such as TextBox1, Command2, etc.
   (C) Have special meaning and should not be used while naming variables.
   (D) Are used as prefixes for control names (such as txt, btn, lbl, and lst).

8. To continue a long statement on another line, use:
   - (A) An underscore character
   - (B) An ampersand character
   - (C) Ctrl + Enter.
   - (D) A space followed by an underscore character.

9. What is the proper syntax for using a message dialog box?
   - (A) MessageBox.Show("Hi there", "Hi")
   - (B) MessageBox.Show(Hi there, Hi)
   - (C) MessageBox.Show "Hi There", "Hi"
   - (D) MessageBox.Show Hi There, Hi

10. What will be the output of the following statement?

    txtBox.Text = Format Currcy(1234.567)

    - (A) $1234.567
    - (B) 1,234.57
    - (C) $1234.57
    - (D) $1,234.57

11. Asc("A") is 65. What is Asc("C")?
    - (A) 66
    - (B) 67
    - (C) 68
    - (D) "C"

12. Asc("A") is 65. What is displayed by txtBox.Text = Chr(65) & "BC"?
    - (A) ABC
    - (B) A BC
    - (C) 656667
    - (D) Not enough information is available.

13. Which of the following expressions has its value the words "Hello World" surrounded by quotation marks?
    - (A) "Hello World"
    - (B) Chr(34) & "Hello World"
    - (C) Chr(34) & Hello World & Chr(34)
    - (D) Chr(34) & "Hello World" & Chr(34)

14. Which of the following is true?
    - (A) "Cat" = "cat"
    - (B) "Cat" < "cat"
    - (C) "Cat" > "cat"
    - (D) Relational operators are only valid for numeric values.

15. Which of the following is a valid Visual Basic conditional statement?
    - (A) 2 < n < 5
    - (B) 2 < n Or < 5
    - (C) 2 < n Or 5
    - (D) (2 < n) Or (n < 5)

16. The three main logical operators are______, ______, and ______.
    - (A) And, Or, Not
    - (B) And, Not, If
    - (C) Or, Not, If
    - (D) False, And, True

17. Which value for x would make the following condition true: x > = 5?
    - (A) x is equal to 7
    - (B) x is equal to 5
    - (C) x is equal to 5.001
    - (D) all of these

18. Which value for x would make the following condition true: Not (x >= 5)
    - (A) X is equal to 7
    - (B) X is equal to 4
    - (C) X is equal to 5.001
    - (D) X is equal to 5.001

19. Constructs in which an If block is contained inside another If block are called:
    - (A) Multi-If blocks
    - (B) Nested If blocks
    - (C) Sequential If blocks
    - (D) None of the above

20. Suppose that the selector in a Select Case block is the string variable myVar. Which of the following is NOT a valid Case clause?
    - (A) Case "Adams"
    - (B) Case "739"
    - (C) Case (myVar.Substring(0, 1))
    - (D) Case myVar.Length

21. Different items appearing in the same value list of a Select Case block must be separated by a ______.

(A) Semi colon

(B) Comma

(C) Colon

(D) Pair of quotation marks

22. Which case clause will be true whenever the value of the selector in a Select Case block is between 1 and 5 or is 8?

(A) Case 1 To 8   (B) Case 1 To 5, 8

(C) Case 1 To 8, 5   (D) Case 1 To 5; 8

23. Which case clause will be true whenever the value of the selector in a Select Case block is greater than or equal to 7?

(A) Case Is >7   (B) Case Is = 8

(C) Case Is >= 7   (D) Case Is <= 8

24. Which type of items are valid for use in value list of a case clause?

(A) Literals   (B) Variables

(C) Expressions   (D) All of these

25. What happens to a variable declared locally inside a Sub procedure after the procedure terminates?

(A) It maintains its value even after the End Sub statement executes.

(B) It ceases to exist after the End Sub statement executes.

(C) It loses its value temporarily after the End Sub statement executes, but regains that value upon re-entry to the Sub procedure.

(D) It is reset to its default value.

26. Suppose a variable is passed by reference to a parameter of a Sub procedure, and the parameter has its value changed inside the Sub procedure. What will the value of the variable be after the Sub procedure has executed?

(A) It will have the newly modified value from inside the Sub procedure.

(B) Its value can't be determined without more information.

(C) It will retain the value it had before the call to the Sub procedure

(D) None of these

27. The declaration statement for a class-level variable should be placed _______.

(A) Inside an event procedure

(B) Inside a general procedure

(C) Anywhere in the program region, except inside a procedure

(D) Above the statement Public Class frmName

28. Variables declared inside a procedure are said to have _______.

(A) Local scope

(B) Procedure-level scope

(C) Class-level scope

(D) None of these

29. What will be the output of the following program when the button is clicked?

```
Private Sub btnDisplay_Click(...)
Handles btn
Display.Click
Dim number As Double = 3
DoubleAndSquare(number)
txtBox.Text = CStr(number)
End Sub
Sub DoubleAndSquare(ByRef
myVar As Double)
myVar = myVar + myVar
myVar = myVar * myVar
```

(A) 3   (B) 36

(C) 6   (D) 0

30. Suppose the variable myName is declared in a Dim statement in two different Sub procedures. Which statement is true?

(A) The program will malfunction when it is executed.

(B) When the value of myName is changed in one Sub procedure, it will also be changed in the other Sub procedure.

(C) Visual Basic's smart editor will alert you that this is an error before the program is executed.

(D) The two variables will be local to their respective Sub procedures.

31. What would be the value of variable res after execution?

    res = 9 Mod 2+1–2

    (A) –1   (B) 3
    (C) 0   (D) 4

32. The statements which control the flow of execution of a program are called conditional statements. VB provides two conditional statements which are _______.

    (A) If .... Then .... Else and Select Case
    (B) If .... Then .... Else and Do While
    (C) Select Case and For .... Next
    (D) For Next and Do .... Loop

33. What is the output of the following Visual Basic code?

    Print Replace("Hello-World", "-", "/")

    (A) HelloWorld   (B) Hello/World
    (C) Hello World   (D) helloworld

34. Observe the snapshot shown here and identify which of the marked areas when clicked will open the Form Layout window?

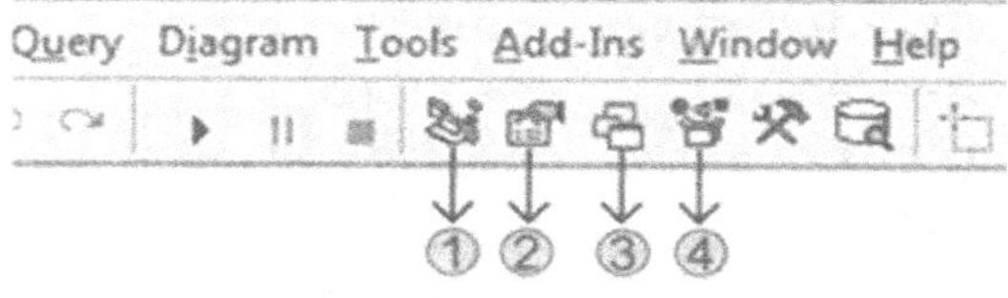

(A) 1   (B) 2
(C) 3   (D) 4

35. Match the components given in Column-I with the functions they provide given in Column-II.

	Column - I		Column - II
(a)	Form window	(i)	To write the instruction for any object.
(b)	Properties window	(ii)	Displays a list of forms and other objects that constitute an application.
(c)	Project Explorer window	(iii)	Used to place various controls on a blank area.
(d)	Code window	(iv)	Used to set the characteristic of forms and other controls placed on them.

(A) (a) - (iv), (b) - (iii), (c) - (i), (d) - (ii)
(B) (a) - (iv), (b) - (i), (c) - (ii), (d) - (iii)
(C) (a) - (iii), (b) - (iv), (c) - (ii), (d) - (i)
(D) (a) - (iv), (b) - (i), (c) - (iii), (d) - (ii)

—Darken Your Choice with HB Pencil—

1. Ⓐ Ⓑ Ⓒ Ⓓ	8. Ⓐ Ⓑ Ⓒ Ⓓ	15. Ⓐ Ⓑ Ⓒ Ⓓ	22 Ⓐ Ⓑ Ⓒ Ⓓ	29. Ⓐ Ⓑ Ⓒ Ⓓ
2. Ⓐ Ⓑ Ⓒ Ⓓ	9. Ⓐ Ⓑ Ⓒ Ⓓ	16. Ⓐ Ⓑ Ⓒ Ⓓ	23. Ⓐ Ⓑ Ⓒ Ⓓ	30. Ⓐ Ⓑ Ⓒ Ⓓ
3. Ⓐ Ⓑ Ⓒ Ⓓ	10. Ⓐ Ⓑ Ⓒ Ⓓ	17. Ⓐ Ⓑ Ⓒ Ⓓ	24. Ⓐ Ⓑ Ⓒ Ⓓ	31. Ⓐ Ⓑ Ⓒ Ⓓ
4. Ⓐ Ⓑ Ⓒ Ⓓ	11. Ⓐ Ⓑ Ⓒ Ⓓ	18. Ⓐ Ⓑ Ⓒ Ⓓ	25. Ⓐ Ⓑ Ⓒ Ⓓ	32. Ⓐ Ⓑ Ⓒ Ⓓ
5. Ⓐ Ⓑ Ⓒ Ⓓ	12. Ⓐ Ⓑ Ⓒ Ⓓ	19. Ⓐ Ⓑ Ⓒ Ⓓ	26. Ⓐ Ⓑ Ⓒ Ⓓ	33. Ⓐ Ⓑ Ⓒ Ⓓ
6. Ⓐ Ⓑ Ⓒ Ⓓ	13. Ⓐ Ⓑ Ⓒ Ⓓ	20. Ⓐ Ⓑ Ⓒ Ⓓ	27. Ⓐ Ⓑ Ⓒ Ⓓ	34. Ⓐ Ⓑ Ⓒ Ⓓ
7. Ⓐ Ⓑ Ⓒ Ⓓ	14. Ⓐ Ⓑ Ⓒ Ⓓ	21. Ⓐ Ⓑ Ⓒ Ⓓ	28. Ⓐ Ⓑ Ⓒ Ⓓ	35. Ⓐ Ⓑ Ⓒ Ⓓ

HTML AND CSS

LEARNING OBJECTIVES

➤ Basics of HTML
➤ Different HTML Tags

MULTIPLE CHOICE QUESTIONS

1. _______ connects web pages.
   (A) Connector   (B) Link
   (C) Hyperlink   (D) None of these

2. Internet is _______.
   (A) A network of networks
   (B) An ocean of resources waiting to be mined
   (C) A cooperative anarchy
   (D) All of these

3. ___________ is suitable for remote administration of a computer.
   (A) FTP
   (B) Shell
   (C) Remote Procedure Call
   (D) Telnet

4. Title tag is nested within the _______ tag.
   (A) Body   (B) Head
   (C) List   (D) Table

5. _______ is a web's native protocol.
   (A) SLIP   (B) TCP/IP
   (C) HTTP   (D) PPP

6. The Internet uses the _______ as the protocol engine.
   (A) SLIP   (B) HTTP
   (C) TCP/IP   (D) PPP

7. A _______ is a symbolic name a network administrator assigns to a machine.
   (A) URL   (B) DNS
   (C) IP address   (D) Host name

8. Which of the following protocol is used for e-mail services?
   (A) SMAP   (B) SMTP
   (C) SMIP   (D) SMOP

9. _______ is the incoming e-mail server.
   (A) POP   (B) SMTP
   (C) SMIP   (D) PPP

10. _______ is a uniform naming scheme for locating resources on the web.
    (A) URL
    (B) HTTP
    (C) WEBNAME
    (D) RESOURCENAME

11. The attribute _______ of <BODY> tag sets color of hypertext links.
    (A) Link   (B) Vlink
    (C) Alink   (D) Hlink

12. Default font size of HTML is _______.
    (A) 2   (B) 4
    (C) 6   (D) 3

13. This is a networking device that passes data between networks having similar functions but dissimilar implementations.
    (A) Hub   (B) Modem
    (C) Gateway   (D) Repeater

14. In order to connect to ISP's server, you need ______.
    (A) Hand gloves
    (B) Printer
    (C) User name and Password
    (D) None of these

15. DNS translates ______.
    (A) Domain name into IP
    (B) IP into domain name
    (C) Both (A) and (B)
    (D) Domain name into physical address

16. In order to upload an HTML file to a web server, you use
    (A) HTTP   (B) SMTP
    (C) SIP   (D) FTP

17. IEEE stands for ______.
    (A) Institute of Estimated Elevator Efficiency
    (B) Institute of Electrical and Economical Engineers
    (C) Institute of Eurasia Engineering Event
    (D) Institute of Electrical and Electronics Engineers

18. The regional networks connected to the corporate networks are also called ______.
    (A) Backbone
    (B) LAN COM
    (C) WAN COM
    (D) Intranet

19. Once an email is sent, the message is broken into pieces called ______.
    (A) Packets
    (B) Process
    (C) Digits
    (D) Bytes

20. ________ is known as the father of World Wide Web.
    (A) Robert Cailliau
    (B) Tim Thompson
    (C) Charles Darwin
    (D) Tim Berners-Lee

HOTS (ACHIEVERS SECTION)

21. Consider the statement given here.

```
<a href = "http://www.yahoo.com/">Link</a>
   (1)             (2)              (3)  (4)
```

Which of the parts marked by numbers (1), (2), (3) and (4) would get displayed in the webpage?
    (A) 1   (B) 2
    (C) 3   (D) 4

22. What would be the output of the given HTML code?

```
<HTML>
<hr size=4 color=black width=50%>
<h1 align=center> COMPUTER WORLD </h1>
<hr size=4 color=black width=50%>
</HTML>
```

    (A) COMPUTER WORLD
    (B) COMPUTER WORLD
    (C) COMPUTER WORLD
    (D) COMPUTER WORLD

23. If you use ________, by default the items will be displayed in bulleted form.
   (A) <bl> and </bl>
   (B) <b> and </b>
   (C) <li> and </li>
   (D) <th> and </th>

24. To convert the text "Navneet Mehra", to a hyperlink to www.navneetmehra.com, use ________.
   (A) <a>http://www.navneetmehra.com</a>
   (B) <a href="http://www.navneetmehra.com"> Navneet Mehra</a>
   (C) <a name="http://www.navneetmehra.com"> navneetmehra.com</a>
   (D) <a url="http://www.navneetmehra.com"> Navneet Mehra</a>

25. The img tag is used for displaying an image in a webpage. The correct use of the img tag is __________.
   (A) <img src="imagename.format" alt="This is an image" height="45" width="45">"
   (B) </img src="imageurl.html"><alt="This is an image", height="45", width="45"/>
   (C) <image src="imagename.gif, alt="This is an image"><height="45">, <width="45"/>
   (D) <img="imagename.format" height="45", width="45">

🕐🕐🕐

1.	Ⓐ Ⓑ Ⓒ Ⓓ	6.	Ⓐ Ⓑ Ⓒ Ⓓ	11.	Ⓐ Ⓑ Ⓒ Ⓓ	16	Ⓐ Ⓑ Ⓒ Ⓓ	21.	Ⓐ Ⓑ Ⓒ Ⓓ
2.	Ⓐ Ⓑ Ⓒ Ⓓ	7.	Ⓐ Ⓑ Ⓒ Ⓓ	12.	Ⓐ Ⓑ Ⓒ Ⓓ	17.	Ⓐ Ⓑ Ⓒ Ⓓ	22.	Ⓐ Ⓑ Ⓒ Ⓓ
3.	Ⓐ Ⓑ Ⓒ Ⓓ	8.	Ⓐ Ⓑ Ⓒ Ⓓ	13.	Ⓐ Ⓑ Ⓒ Ⓓ	18.	Ⓐ Ⓑ Ⓒ Ⓓ	23.	Ⓐ Ⓑ Ⓒ Ⓓ
4.	Ⓐ Ⓑ Ⓒ Ⓓ	9.	Ⓐ Ⓑ Ⓒ Ⓓ	14.	Ⓐ Ⓑ Ⓒ Ⓓ	19.	Ⓐ Ⓑ Ⓒ Ⓓ	24.	Ⓐ Ⓑ Ⓒ Ⓓ
5.	Ⓐ Ⓑ Ⓒ Ⓓ	10.	Ⓐ Ⓑ Ⓒ Ⓓ	15.	Ⓐ Ⓑ Ⓒ Ⓓ	20.	Ⓐ Ⓑ Ⓒ Ⓓ	25.	Ⓐ Ⓑ Ⓒ Ⓓ

MS WORD

LEARNING OBJECTIVES

➤ Usage of MS Word
➤ Shortcut commands for MS Word

MULTIPLE CHOICE QUESTIONS

1. Which option in File menu is used to close a file in MS Word?
   (A) New
   (B) Quit
   (C) Close
   (D) Exit

2. Which bar is usually located below the Title Bar that provides categorized options?
   (A) Menu bar
   (B) Status Bar
   (C) Tool bar
   (D) Scroll bar

3. Which of these toolbars allow changing of fonts and their sizes?
   (A) Standard
   (B) Formatting
   (C) Print Preview
   (D) None of these

4. Which key should be pressed to start a new paragraph in MS Word?
   (A) Down Cursor Key
   (B) Enter Key
   (C) Shift + Enter
   (D) Ctrl + Enter

5. Which menu in MS Word can be used to change the size and typeface of a character?
   (A) View
   (B) Tools
   (C) Format
   (D) Data

6. On which page is the header or the footer printed by default?
   (A) On first page
   (B) On alternate page
   (C) On every page
   (D) None of these

7. What is the use of a ruler in MS Word?
   (A) To set tabs
   (B) To set indents
   (C) To change page margins
   (D) All of these

8. Using Find command in Word, we can search ______.
   (A) Characters
   (B) Formats
   (C) Symbols
   (D) All of these

9. MS Word automatically moves the text to the next line when it reaches the right edge of the screen. This is called ______.
   (A) Carriage Return
   (B) Enter
   (C) Word Wrap
   (D) None of these

10. To select a text means to select
    (A) A word
    (B) An entire sentence
    (C) Whole document
    (D) Any of these

11. Single spacing in MS Word document causes ______ point line spacing.
    (A) 10
    (B) 12
    (C) 14
    (D) 16

12. What would you choose to display the statistics about a document?
    (A) Tools, word count
    (B) Insert, statistics
    (C) Tools, spelling and grammar
    (D) Tools, statistics

13. Which feature do you use to create a newspaper like document?
    (A) Bullets and numbering
    (B) Tables
    (C) Columns
    (D) Tab stops

14. What would you choose to list synonyms and antonyms of a selected word?
    (A) Tools, Spelling & Grammar
    (B) Tools, Language
    (C) Tools, Options
    (D) Insert, Cross-reference

15. Which language does MS Word use to create Macros?
    (A) Visual C++
    (B) Visual Basic
    (C) FoxPro
    (D) Access

16. What do you call 'a collection of character and paragraph formatting commands'?
    (A) The defaults
    (B) A template
    (C) A style
    (D) A boilerplate

17. In MS Word, Ctrl+S is for ______.
    (A) Scenarios
    (B) Size
    (C) Saving
    (D) Checking Spellings

18. Which key is used to increase left indent?
    (A) Ctrl+I
    (B) Ctrl+M
    (C) Alt+I
    (D) F10

19. Which key is used to select all the text in the document?
    (A) Ctrl+T
    (B) Ctrl+A
    (C) Ctrl+F
    (D) Ctrl+N

20. To undo the last work, press
    (A) Ctrl+U
    (B) Ctrl+Y
    (C) Ctrl+Z
    (D) Ctrl+W

21. Which feature enables us to send the same letter to different persons?
    (A) Macros
    (B) Template
    (C) Mail merge
    (D) None

22. Which key deletes the character to the left of the cursor?
    (A) End
    (B) Backspace
    (C) Home
    (D) Delete

23. Which key deletes the character to the right of the cursor?
    (A) End
    (B) Backspace
    (C) Home
    (D) Delete

24. How would you save a document with a new name?
    (A) Press Ctrl+S
    (B) Click File, Save
    (C) Click Tools, Options, Save
    (D) Click File, Save As

25. How would you move selected text from one place to another?
    (A) Move and Paste
    (B) Copy and Paste
    (C) Cut and Paste
    (D) Delete and Paste

26. How do you magnify your document?
    (A) View, Zoom
    (B) Format, Font
    (C) Tools, Options
    (D) Tools, Customize

27. Which feature enables you to move directly to specific location in a document?
(A) Subdocuments
(B) Bookmarks
(C) Cross-references
(D) Outlines

28. What is inserted as cross-reference in MS Word?
(A) Placeholders
(B) Bookmarks
(C) Objects
(D) Word fields

29. Which keystroke is used for updating a field?
(A) F6   (B) F9
(C) F11   (D) F12

30. A master document contains _______, each of which contains a pointer to a file on a disc.
(A) Placeholders
(B) Subdocuments
(C) Bookmarks
(D) References

HOTS (ACHIEVERS SECTION)

31. Which of the following steps will allow you to combine multiple versions of a document?
(A) Review tab → Compare group → click on drop-down arrow of 'Compare' → click on 'Combine'
(B) Review tab → Changes group → click on drop-down arrow of 'Changes' → click on 'Combine'
(C) Review tab → Changes group → click on 'Merge'
(D) Review tab → Changes group → click on drop-down arrow of 'Combine' → select versions of document → click on 'Combine'

32. What would happen when you perform the following steps in a document?

Go to Review tab → Tracking Group → Show Markup → Uncheck "Formatting" option
(A) It will disable the formatting option available on the ribbon.
(B) It will remove all the formatting applied to the document leaving only the plain text.
(C) It will hide formatting changes which were made to the document when Track Changes option was enabled.
(D) Both (A) and (B)

33. Which of the following MS-Word features will save information in every few minutes so that you do not lose data?
(A) AutoPreserve
(B) AutoPrevent Save
(C) AutoRecover
(D) AutoSave

34. Which of the following properties can be checked using Inspect document feature available in File tab?
(i) Revision marks such as comments
(ii) Author name
(iii) Header, footer or watermarks
(A) Only (i)
(B) Only (ii)
(C) Only (iii)
(D) All (i), (ii) and (iii)

35. Swati is making a document in MS-Word and now she wants to insert an image,

in such a way that whatever changes she makes to source file of image, shall reflect in Word also. However, she does not want that if the original file is deleted, the image from Word document also gets deleted. Which of the following options she should select to achieve this?

(A) Insert tab →Illustrations group → Picture → click on Insert dropdown arrow → Insert.

(B) Insert tab → Illustrations group → Picture → click on Insert dropdown arrow → Link to File.

(C) Insert tab → Illustrations group → Picture → click on Insert dropdown arrow → Insert and Link.

(D) Insert tab → Illustrations group → Picture → click on Insert dropdown arrow → Image.

	A B C D		A B C D		A B C D		A B C D		A B C D
1.	Ⓐ Ⓑ Ⓒ Ⓓ	8.	Ⓐ Ⓑ Ⓒ Ⓓ	15.	Ⓐ Ⓑ Ⓒ Ⓓ	22	Ⓐ Ⓑ Ⓒ Ⓓ	29.	Ⓐ Ⓑ Ⓒ Ⓓ
2.	Ⓐ Ⓑ Ⓒ Ⓓ	9.	Ⓐ Ⓑ Ⓒ Ⓓ	16.	Ⓐ Ⓑ Ⓒ Ⓓ	23.	Ⓐ Ⓑ Ⓒ Ⓓ	30.	Ⓐ Ⓑ Ⓒ Ⓓ
3.	Ⓐ Ⓑ Ⓒ Ⓓ	10.	Ⓐ Ⓑ Ⓒ Ⓓ	17.	Ⓐ Ⓑ Ⓒ Ⓓ	24.	Ⓐ Ⓑ Ⓒ Ⓓ	31.	Ⓐ Ⓑ Ⓒ Ⓓ
4.	Ⓐ Ⓑ Ⓒ Ⓓ	11.	Ⓐ Ⓑ Ⓒ Ⓓ	18.	Ⓐ Ⓑ Ⓒ Ⓓ	25.	Ⓐ Ⓑ Ⓒ Ⓓ	32.	Ⓐ Ⓑ Ⓒ Ⓓ
5.	Ⓐ Ⓑ Ⓒ Ⓓ	12.	Ⓐ Ⓑ Ⓒ Ⓓ	19.	Ⓐ Ⓑ Ⓒ Ⓓ	26.	Ⓐ Ⓑ Ⓒ Ⓓ	33.	Ⓐ Ⓑ Ⓒ Ⓓ
6.	Ⓐ Ⓑ Ⓒ Ⓓ	13.	Ⓐ Ⓑ Ⓒ Ⓓ	20.	Ⓐ Ⓑ Ⓒ Ⓓ	27.	Ⓐ Ⓑ Ⓒ Ⓓ	34.	Ⓐ Ⓑ Ⓒ Ⓓ
7.	Ⓐ Ⓑ Ⓒ Ⓓ	14.	Ⓐ Ⓑ Ⓒ Ⓓ	21.	Ⓐ Ⓑ Ⓒ Ⓓ	28.	Ⓐ Ⓑ Ⓒ Ⓓ	35.	Ⓐ Ⓑ Ⓒ Ⓓ

MS EXCEL

LEARNING OBJECTIVES

➤ Usage of MS Excel
➤ Shortcut commands for MS Excel

MULTIPLE CHOICE QUESTIONS

1. Comments put in cells are called
   (A) Smart Tip   (B) Cell Tip
   (C) Web Tip   (D) Soft Tip

2. Comments can be added to cells using
   _____.
   (A) Edit ⇒ Comments
   (B) Insert ⇒ Comment
   (C) File ⇒ Comments
   (D) View ⇒ Comments

3. Which menu option can be used to split windows into two?
   (A) Format ⇒ Window
   (B) View ⇒ Window ⇒ Split
   (C) Window ⇒ Split
   (D) View ⇒ Split

4. Getting data from a cell located in a different sheet is called
   (A) Accessing   (B) Referencing
   (C) Updating   (D) Functioning

5. Which of the following is not a valid data type in Excel?
   (A) Number   (B) Character
   (C) Label   (D) Date/Time

6. Which elements of a worksheet can be protected from accidental modification?
   (A) Contents   (B) Objects
   (C) Scenarios   (D) All of these

7. A numeric value can be treated as label value if _____ precedes it.
   (A) Apostrophe (')   (B) Exclamation (!)
   (C) Hash (#)   (D) Tilde (~)

8. Concatenation of text can be done using
   (A) Apostrophe (')
   (B) Exclamation (!)
   (C) Hash (#)
   (D) Ampersand (&)

9. Which area in an Excel sheet allows entry of values and formulas?
   (A) Title Bar
   (B) Menu Bar
   (C) Formula Bar
   (D) Standard Tool Bar

10. Multiple calculations can be made in a single formula using _____.
    (A) Standard Formulas
    (B) Array Formula
    (C) Complex Formulas
    (D) Smart Formula

11. An Excel Workbook is a collection of
    _____.
    (A) Workbooks
    (B) Worksheets
    (C) Charts
    (D) Worksheets and Charts

12. What do you mean by a Workspace?
(A) Group of Columns
(B) Group of Worksheets
(C) Group of Rows
(D) Group of Workbooks

13. MS EXCEL is based on ______.
(A) WINDOWS   (B) DOS
(C) UNIX   (D) OS/2

14. In EXCEL, you can sum a large range of data by simply selecting a tool button called ____.
(A) AutoFill   (B) Auto correct
(C) Auto sum   (D) Auto format

15. To select an entire column in MS EXCEL, press
(A) CTRL + C
(B) CTRL + Arrow key
(C) CTRL + S
(D) None of these

16. To return the remainder after a number is divided by a divisor in EXCEL, we use the function
(A) ROUND ( )   (B) FACT ( )
(C) MOD ( )   (D) DIV ( )

17. Which function is not available in the Consolidate dialog box?
(A) Pmt
(B) Average
(C) Max
(D) Sum

18. Which is not the function of "Edit, Clear" command?
(A) Delete contents
(B) Delete notes
(C) Delete cells
(D) Delete formats

19. Microsoft Excel is a powerful __________.
(A) Word processing package
(B) Spreadsheet package
(C) Communication S/W Package
(D) DBMS package

20. How do you rearrange the data in ascending or descending order?
(A) Data, Sort   (B) Data, Form
(C) Data, Table   (D) Data Subtotals

21. Which chart can be created in Excel?
(A) Area   (B) Line
(C) Pie   (D) All of these

22. What will be the output if you format the cell containing 5436.8 as '#,##0.00'?
(A) 5,430.00   (B) 5,436.80
(C) 5,436.8   (D) 6.8

23. How do you display current date and time in MS Excel?
(A) Date ()   (B) Today ()
(C) Now ()   (D) Time ()

24. How do you display current date in MS Excel?
(A) Date ()   (B) Today ()
(C) Now ()   (D) Time ()

25. How do you wrap the text in a cell?
(A) Format, cells, font
(B) Format, cells, protection
(C) Format, cells, number
(D) Format, cells, alignment

26. What does COUNT () function do?
(A) Counts cells having alphabets
(B) Counts empty cells
(C) Counts cells having number
(D) Counts non-empty cells

27. What is the short cut key to highlight the entire column?
(A) Ctrl+C   (B) Ctrl+Enter
(C) Ctrl+Page Up   (D) Ctrl+Space Bar

28. In the formula, which symbol specifies the fixed columns or rows?
(A) $ (B) *
(C) %   (D) &

29. Excel displays the current cell address in the ________.
(A) Formula bar   (B) Status Bar
(C) Name Box   (D) Title Bar

30. What is the correct way to refer the cell A10 on sheet 3 from sheet 1?
(A) Sheet3!A10
(B) Sheet1!A10
(C) Sheet3.A10
(D) A10

31. Presence of dollar sign ($) before a row and column number, in a cell range for example, $C$7:$D$10 indicates that __________.

    (A) An absolute cell reference is created
    (B) Cell address will change when it is copied to another cell
    (C) The sheet tab is changed
    (D) The status bar does not display the cell address

32. Which of the following options would replace the "?" to open the Watch Window?

    Formulas tab→ ? → Watch Window

    (A) Calculations
    (B) Function
    (C) Formula Auditing
    (D) Data Tools

33. Which of the following statements is INCORRECT about 'Share Workbook' feature?

    (A) It allows multiple people to work in a workbook at the same time.
    (B) It requires workbook to be saved to a network location.
    (C) Workbook that contains tables can be shared.
    (D) Both (A) and (B)

34. Rishab wants to add a condition to selected range of cells, such that when a user enters a value less than 0, it should display a message stating that only positive numbers can be entered. Which of the following can be used for this purpose?

    (A) Consolidate
    (B) Data Validation
    (C) Data Restriction
    (D) What-lf Analysis

35. An organization sells its products in three regions and the quarterly sales from each region is stored in three identical worksheets. Now, the sales team want to know the total sales of each product by adding sales from all regions. Which MS-Excel tool should be used for this purpose?

    (A) Goal Seek   (B) Consolidate
    (C) Watch Window   (D) Subtotal

Darken Your Choice with HB Pencil

1.	Ⓐ Ⓑ Ⓒ Ⓓ	8.	Ⓐ Ⓑ Ⓒ Ⓓ	15.	Ⓐ Ⓑ Ⓒ Ⓓ	22	Ⓐ Ⓑ Ⓒ Ⓓ	29.	Ⓐ Ⓑ Ⓒ Ⓓ
2.	Ⓐ Ⓑ Ⓒ Ⓓ	9.	Ⓐ Ⓑ Ⓒ Ⓓ	16.	Ⓐ Ⓑ Ⓒ Ⓓ	23.	Ⓐ Ⓑ Ⓒ Ⓓ	30.	Ⓐ Ⓑ Ⓒ Ⓓ
3.	Ⓐ Ⓑ Ⓒ Ⓓ	10.	Ⓐ Ⓑ Ⓒ Ⓓ	17.	Ⓐ Ⓑ Ⓒ Ⓓ	24.	Ⓐ Ⓑ Ⓒ Ⓓ	31.	Ⓐ Ⓑ Ⓒ Ⓓ
4.	Ⓐ Ⓑ Ⓒ Ⓓ	11.	Ⓐ Ⓑ Ⓒ Ⓓ	18.	Ⓐ Ⓑ Ⓒ Ⓓ	25.	Ⓐ Ⓑ Ⓒ Ⓓ	32.	Ⓐ Ⓑ Ⓒ Ⓓ
5.	Ⓐ Ⓑ Ⓒ Ⓓ	12.	Ⓐ Ⓑ Ⓒ Ⓓ	19.	Ⓐ Ⓑ Ⓒ Ⓓ	26.	Ⓐ Ⓑ Ⓒ Ⓓ	33.	Ⓐ Ⓑ Ⓒ Ⓓ
6.	Ⓐ Ⓑ Ⓒ Ⓓ	13.	Ⓐ Ⓑ Ⓒ Ⓓ	20.	Ⓐ Ⓑ Ⓒ Ⓓ	27.	Ⓐ Ⓑ Ⓒ Ⓓ	34.	Ⓐ Ⓑ Ⓒ Ⓓ
7.	Ⓐ Ⓑ Ⓒ Ⓓ	14.	Ⓐ Ⓑ Ⓒ Ⓓ	21.	Ⓐ Ⓑ Ⓒ Ⓓ	28.	Ⓐ Ⓑ Ⓒ Ⓓ	35.	Ⓐ Ⓑ Ⓒ Ⓓ

MS POWERPOINT

LEARNING OBJECTIVES

➤ Usage of MS Powerpoint
➤ Shortcut commands for MS Powerpoint

MULTIPLE CHOICE QUESTIONS

1. PowerPoint presentation is a collection of ______.
   (A) Slides and handouts
   (B) Speaker's notes
   (C) Outlines
   (D) All of these

2. How can a slide show be repeated continuously?
   (A) Loop continuously until 'Esc'
   (B) Repeat continuously
   (C) Loop more
   (D) None

3. From where can we set the timing for each object?
   (A) Slide show, custom transition
   (B) Slide show, Slide transition
   (C) Slide show, custom animation
   (D) View, slide sorter

4. The arrangement of elements such as title and subtitle text, pictures, tables etc., is called:
   (A) Layout
   (B) Presentation
   (C) Design
   (D) Scheme

5. A file which contains readymade styles that can be used for a presentation is called:
   (A) AutoStyle
   (B) Template
   (C) Wizard
   (D) Pre-formatting

6. After choosing a predefined template, which option helps you change the background color?
   (A) Design Template
   (B) Color Scheme
   (C) Animation Scheme
   (D) Color Effects

7. Ellipse motion is a pre-defined ______.
   (A) Design Template
   (B) Color Scheme
   (C) Animation Scheme
   (D) None of these

8. Animation schemes can be applied to ______ in the presentation.
   (A) All slides
   (B) Select slides
   (C) Current slide
   (D) All of these

9. To insert new slide in the current presentation, we can choose:
   (A) Ctrl+M   (B) Ctrl+N
   (C) Ctrl+O   (D) Ctrl+F

10. To open the existing presentation, press
    (A) Ctrl + L   (B) Ctrl + N
    (C) Ctrl + A   (D) Ctrl + O

11. Slides can have
    (A) Title, text, graphs
    (B) Drawn objects, shapes
    (C) Clipart, drawn art, visual
    (D) All of these

12. A chart can be put as a part of the presentation using
    (A) Insert ⇒ Pictures ⇒ Chart
    (B) Insert ⇒ Chart
    (C) Edit ⇒ Chart
    (D) View ⇒ Chart

13. We can replace font on all slides with another font using the option
    (A) Edit ⇒ Fonts
    (B) Tools ⇒ Fonts
    (C) Tools ⇒ Replace Fonts
    (D) Format ⇒ Replace Fonts

14. Which key on the keyboard can be used to view Slide Show?
    (A) F1   (B) F2
    (C) F5   (D) F10

15. Which option in PowerPoint allows you to create a package of your presentation to be shown in another computer?
    (A) Save As
    (B) Save and Go
    (C) Pack and Go
    (D) Web and Go

16. Which view in PowerPoint can be used to enter speaker comments?
    (A) Normal
    (B) Slide Show
    (C) Slide Sorter
    (D) Notes Page view

17. Which option can be used to set custom timings for slides in a presentation?
    (A) Slider Timings
    (B) Slider Timer
    (C) Rehearsal
    (D) Slide Show Setup

18. Which option can be used to create a new slide show with the current slides but in a different order?
    (A) Rehearsal
    (B) Custom Slide show
    (C) Slide Show Setup
    (D) Slide Show View

19. Which of the following is an example of Automatic text formatting?
    (A) Underlining Hyperlink
    (B) Adjusting extra space
    (C) Replacing two – s with a hyphen
    (D) All of these

20. PowerPoint can display data from which of the following add-in software of MS Office?
    (A) Equation Editor
    (B) Organization Chart
    (C) Photo Album
    (D) All of these

21. The Spelling dialog box can be opened by choosing spelling from the _______ menu.
    (A) Insert   (B) File
    (C) Tools   (D) View

22. Which key should you press to check spelling?
    (A) F3   (B) F5
    (C) F7   (D) F9

23. Which PowerPoint feature allows the user to create a simple presentation without having to spend too much time on it?
    (A) AutoContent Wizard
    (B) Animation

(C) Color Schemes

(D) Chart Wizard

24. Which PowerPoint feature adds special effects to modify the appearance of the slides and the timing between each slide?
 (A) Color Schemes
 (B) Animation
 (C) Transition Settings
 (D) Handouts

25. Slide sorter view of PowerPoint is available on ______ menu.
 (A) Insert (B) File
 (C) View (D) Edit

26. To print the PowerPoint presentation, press
 (A) Ctrl + T (B) Ctrl + E
 (C) Ctrl + S (D) Ctrl + P

27. What is a slide transition?
 (A) Overheads
 (B) Letters
 (C) A special effect used to introduce a slide in a slide show
 (D) The way one slide looks

28. What does "apply design template" do?
 (A) Changes the content of the slide
 (B) Adds functionality to the slide
 (C) Changes the look of the slide without changing the content
 (D) None of these

29. How can you stop a slide show?
 (A) Press the right arrow
 (B) Press Escape
 (C) Press the left arrow
 (D) Press the down arrow

30. What do you do to start the slide show?
 (A) Click on Go
 (B) Turn on transition
 (C) Click on the Slide Show icon
 (D) All of these

HOTS (ACHIEVERS SECTION)

31. If you have two copies of your presentation with some changes in both, you can combine the copy with your original presentation, and then accept or discard changes into the presentation. Which of the following features of PowerPoint will allow you to do this?
 (A) Track Changes
 (B) Document Inspector
 (C) Compare
 (D) Custom Animation

32. Which of the following steps is CORRECT to package a presentation for CD?
 (A) File → Save & Pack → File Types → Package Presentation for CD
 (B) File → Save & Pack → File Types → Publish Slides
 (C) File → Save & Send → File Types → Package Presentation for CD
 (D) File → Save & Go → File Types → Package Presentation for CD

33. In MS-PowerPoint, while typing in a placeholder ______________ option button automatically decreases the size of the font to fit it in the placeholder.
 (A) Text
 (B) Auto Adjust
 (C) AutoFill
 (D) AutoFit Text to Placeholder

34. What is the main functional difference between the Notes Master and Handout Master views?

    (A) You cannot move or resize slide placeholders on the Handout Master, whereas in Notes Master you can.

    (B) In the Notes Master, you cannot format the slide placeholders, whereas in Handout Master you can.

    (C) You cannot format Header placeholder in the Handout Master, whereas in Notes Master you can.

    (D) You cannot change the slide orientation in the Handout Master, whereas in Handout Master you can.

35. What is Legend in a chart?

    (A) A formatting feature for chart title.

    (B) A little box next to chart that describes what the different colors or patterns mean.

    (C) Text that defines the category or the unit of measurement on an axis.

    (D) Text that typically appears above the chart.

1.	Ⓐ Ⓑ Ⓒ Ⓓ	8.	Ⓐ Ⓑ Ⓒ Ⓓ	15.	Ⓐ Ⓑ Ⓒ Ⓓ	22	Ⓐ Ⓑ Ⓒ Ⓓ	29.	Ⓐ Ⓑ Ⓒ Ⓓ
2.	Ⓐ Ⓑ Ⓒ Ⓓ	9.	Ⓐ Ⓑ Ⓒ Ⓓ	16.	Ⓐ Ⓑ Ⓒ Ⓓ	23.	Ⓐ Ⓑ Ⓒ Ⓓ	30.	Ⓐ Ⓑ Ⓒ Ⓓ
3.	Ⓐ Ⓑ Ⓒ Ⓓ	10.	Ⓐ Ⓑ Ⓒ Ⓓ	17.	Ⓐ Ⓑ Ⓒ Ⓓ	24.	Ⓐ Ⓑ Ⓒ Ⓓ	31.	Ⓐ Ⓑ Ⓒ Ⓓ
4.	Ⓐ Ⓑ Ⓒ Ⓓ	11.	Ⓐ Ⓑ Ⓒ Ⓓ	18.	Ⓐ Ⓑ Ⓒ Ⓓ	25.	Ⓐ Ⓑ Ⓒ Ⓓ	32.	Ⓐ Ⓑ Ⓒ Ⓓ
5.	Ⓐ Ⓑ Ⓒ Ⓓ	12.	Ⓐ Ⓑ Ⓒ Ⓓ	19.	Ⓐ Ⓑ Ⓒ Ⓓ	26.	Ⓐ Ⓑ Ⓒ Ⓓ	33.	Ⓐ Ⓑ Ⓒ Ⓓ
6.	Ⓐ Ⓑ Ⓒ Ⓓ	13.	Ⓐ Ⓑ Ⓒ Ⓓ	20.	Ⓐ Ⓑ Ⓒ Ⓓ	27.	Ⓐ Ⓑ Ⓒ Ⓓ	34.	Ⓐ Ⓑ Ⓒ Ⓓ
7.	Ⓐ Ⓑ Ⓒ Ⓓ	14.	Ⓐ Ⓑ Ⓒ Ⓓ	21.	Ⓐ Ⓑ Ⓒ Ⓓ	28.	Ⓐ Ⓑ Ⓒ Ⓓ	35.	Ⓐ Ⓑ Ⓒ Ⓓ

INTERNET AND VIRUSES

LEARNING OBJECTIVES

➤ Fundamental concepts of Internet
➤ Virus and its different types

MULTIPLE CHOICE QUESTIONS

1. What is internet?
   (A) a single network
   (B) A collection of unrelated computers
   (C) interconnection of local area networks
   (D) interconnection of wide area networks

2. To join the internet, the computer has to be connected to a __________
   (A) internet architecture board
   (B) internet society
   (C) internet service provider
   (D) different computer

3. Internet access by transmitting digital data over the wires of a local telephone network is provided by _______
   (A) leased line
   (B) digital subscriber line
   (C) digital signal line
   (D) digital leased line

4. ISP exchanges internet traffic between their networks by __________
   (A) internet exchange point
   (B) subscriber end point
   (C) isp end point
   (D) internet end point

5. Which of the following protocols is used in the internet?
   (A) HTTP
   (B) DHCP
   (C) DNS
   (D) DNS, HTTP and DHCP

6. The size of an IP address in IPv6 is __________
   (A) 32 bits   (B) 64 bits
   (C) 128 bits   (D) 265 bits

7. Internet works on _______
   (A) packet switching
   (B) circuit switching
   (C) both packet switching and circuit switching
   (D) data switching

8. Which one of the following is not an application layer protocol used in internet?
   (A) remote procedure call
   (B) internet relay chat
   (C) resource reservation protocol
   (D) local procedure call

9. Which protocol assigns IP address to the client connected in the internet?
   (A) DHCP   (B) IP
   (C) RPC   (D) RSVP

10. Which one of the following is not used in media access control?
    (A) ethernet
    (B) digital subscriber line
    (C) fiber distributed data interface
    (D) packet switching

11. There are _________ types of computer virus.
    (A) 5   (B) 7
    (C) 10   (D) 12

12. Which of the following is not a type of virus?
    (A) Boot sector   (B) Polymorphic
    (C) Multipartite   (D) Trojans

13. A computer _________ is a malicious code which self-replicates by copying itself to other programs.
    (A) program   (B) virus
    (C) application   (D) worm

14. Which of them is not an ideal way of spreading the virus?
    (A) Infected website
    (B) Emails
    (C) Official Antivirus CDs
    (D) USBs

15. In which year Apple II virus came into existence?
    (A) 1979   (B) 1980
    (C) 1981   (D) 1982

16. In mid-1981, the 1st virus for Apple computers with the name _________ came into existence.
    (A) Apple I   (B) Apple II
    (C) Apple III   (D) Apple Virus

17. The virus hides itself from getting detected by ______ different ways.
    (A) 2   (B) 3
    (C) 4   (D) 5

18. _________________ infects the master boot record and it is challenging and a complex task to remove this virus.
    (A) Boot Sector Virus
    (B) Polymorphic
    (C) Multipartite
    (D) Trojans

19. _________________ gets installed & stays hidden in your computer's memory. It stays involved to the specific type of files which it infects.
    (A) Boot Sector Virus
    (B) Direct Action Virus
    (C) Polymorphic Virus
    (D) Multipartite Virus

20. Direct Action Virus is also known as _________
    (A) Non-resident virus
    (B) Boot Sector Virus
    (C) Polymorphic Virus
    (D) Multipartite Virus

21. _________________ infects the executables as well as the boot sectors.
    (A) Non-resident virus
    (B) Boot Sector Virus
    (C) Polymorphic Virus
    (D) Multipartite Virus

22. _________________ are difficult to identify as they keep on changing their type and signature.
    (A) Non-resident virus
    (B) Boot Sector Virus
    (C) Polymorphic Virus
    (D) Multipartite Virus

23. _________________ deletes all the files that it infects.
    (A) Non-resident virus
    (B) Overwrite Virus
    (C) Polymorphic Virus
    (D) Multipartite Virus

24. _____________ is also known as cavity virus.
   (A) Non-resident virus
   (B) Overwrite Virus
   (C) Polymorphic Virus
   (D) Space-filler Virus

25. Which of the below-mentioned reasons do not satisfy the reason why people create a computer virus?
   (A) Research purpose
   (B) Pranks
   (C) Identity theft
   (D) Protection

HOTS (ACHIEVERS SECTION)

26. _____________ infects the executables as well as the boot sectors.
   (A) Non-resident virus
   (B) Boot Sector Virus
   (C) Polymorphic Virus
   (D) Multipartite Virus

27. _____________ are difficult to identify as they keep on changing their type and signature.
   (A) Non-resident virus
   (B) Boot Sector Virus
   (C) Polymorphic Virus
   (D) Multipartite Virus

28. _____________ deletes all the files that it infects.
   (A) Non-resident virus
   (B) Overwrite Virus
   (C) Polymorphic Virus
   (D) Multipartite Virus

29. _____________ is also known as cavity virus.
   (A) Non-resident virus
   (B) Overwrite Virus
   (C) Polymorphic Virus
   (D) Space-filler Virus

30. Which of the below-mentioned reasons do not satisfy the reason why people create a computer virus?
   (A) Research purpose
   (B) Pranks
   (C) Identity theft
   (D) Protection

Darken Your Choice with HB Pencil

1.	Ⓐ Ⓑ Ⓒ Ⓓ	7.	Ⓐ Ⓑ Ⓒ Ⓓ	13.	Ⓐ Ⓑ Ⓒ Ⓓ	19	Ⓐ Ⓑ Ⓒ Ⓓ	25.	Ⓐ Ⓑ Ⓒ Ⓓ
2.	Ⓐ Ⓑ Ⓒ Ⓓ	8.	Ⓐ Ⓑ Ⓒ Ⓓ	14.	Ⓐ Ⓑ Ⓒ Ⓓ	20.	Ⓐ Ⓑ Ⓒ Ⓓ	26.	Ⓐ Ⓑ Ⓒ Ⓓ
3.	Ⓐ Ⓑ Ⓒ Ⓓ	9.	Ⓐ Ⓑ Ⓒ Ⓓ	15.	Ⓐ Ⓑ Ⓒ Ⓓ	21.	Ⓐ Ⓑ Ⓒ Ⓓ	27.	Ⓐ Ⓑ Ⓒ Ⓓ
4.	Ⓐ Ⓑ Ⓒ Ⓓ	10.	Ⓐ Ⓑ Ⓒ Ⓓ	16.	Ⓐ Ⓑ Ⓒ Ⓓ	22.	Ⓐ Ⓑ Ⓒ Ⓓ	28.	Ⓐ Ⓑ Ⓒ Ⓓ
5.	Ⓐ Ⓑ Ⓒ Ⓓ	11.	Ⓐ Ⓑ Ⓒ Ⓓ	17.	Ⓐ Ⓑ Ⓒ Ⓓ	23.	Ⓐ Ⓑ Ⓒ Ⓓ	29.	Ⓐ Ⓑ Ⓒ Ⓓ
6.	Ⓐ Ⓑ Ⓒ Ⓓ	12.	Ⓐ Ⓑ Ⓒ Ⓓ	18.	Ⓐ Ⓑ Ⓒ Ⓓ	24.	Ⓐ Ⓑ Ⓒ Ⓓ	30.	Ⓐ Ⓑ Ⓒ Ⓓ

COMMUNICATION TECHNOLOGY

LEARNING OBJECTIVES

➤ Basics of Networking
➤ Types of Network

➤ Internet and Web browser
➤ Concept of E-mail

MULTIPLE CHOICE QUESTIONS

1. The Internet is a
   (A) Network of networks
   (B) Website
   (C) Host
   (D) Server

2. A _______ is a group of independent computers attached to one another through communication media.
   (A) Internet
   (B) E-mail
   (C) Network
   (D) All of these

3. WAN stands for
   (A) Wide area network
   (B) World area network
   (C) Wonder area network
   (D) None

4. LAN stands for
   (A) Location access network
   (B) Local anti network
   (C) Local area network
   (D) Location area network

5. What is Multiple Access?
   (A) Accessing a computer from multiple locations.
   (B) A kind of network, MAN.
   (C) If the physical links are shared by more than two nodes, it is said to be Multiple Access.
   (D) None of these

6. What is point-point link?
   (A) If the physical links are limited to a pair of nodes, it is said to be point-point link.
   (B) A wire that connects any two points in a network.
   (C) A type of internet access.
   (D) All of these.

7. The computer network is
   (A) Network computer with cable
   (B) Network computer without cable
   (C) Both of these
   (D) None of these

8. FDDI used which type of physical topology?
   (A) Bus   (B) Ring
   (C) Star   (D) Tree

9. FTP stands for
   (A) File transfer protocol
   (B) File transmission protocol
   (C) Form transfer protocol
   (D) Form transmission protocol

10. Ethernet system uses which of the following technology?
   (A) Bus   (B) Ring
   (C) Star   (D) Tree

11. Which of the following are network services?
   (A) File service
   (B) Print service
   (C) Database service
   (D) All of these

12. If all devices are connected to a central hub, then the topology is called
   (A) Bus Topology
   (B) Ring Topology
   (C) Star Topology
   (D) Tree Topology

13. FDDI stands for
   (A) Fiber Distributed Data Interface
   (B) Fiber Data Distributed Interface
   (C) Fiber Dual Distributed Interface
   (D) Fiber Distributed Data Interface

14. Which of the following is an Application Layer service?
   (A) Network virtual terminal
   (B) File transfer, access and management
   (C) Mail service
   (D) All of these

15. Which is the main function of transport layer?
   (A) Node to node delivery
   (B) End to end delivery
   (C) Synchronization
   (D) Updating and maintaining routing tables

16. The ______________ layer change bits into electromagnetic signals.
   (A) Physical
   (B) Transport
   (C) Data Link
   (D) Presentation

17. TCP/IP ______ layer corresponds to the OSI models three layers.
   (A) Application
   (B) Presentation
   (C) Session
   (D) Transport

18. Which of the transport layer protocols is connectionless?
   (A) UDP
   (B) TCP
   (C) FTP
   (D) NVT

19. Which of the following applications allows a user to access and change remote files without actual transfer?
   (A) DNS   (B) FTP
   (C) NFS   (D) Telnet

20. The data unit in the TCP/IP layer is called a
   (A) Message   (B) Segment
   (C) Datagram   (D) Frame

21. DNS can obtain the ________ of host if its domain name is known and vice versa.
   (A) Station address
   (B) IP address
   (C) Port address
   (D) Checksum

22. Devices on one network can communicate with devices on another network via ______
   (A) File Server
   (B) Utility Server
   (C) Printer Server
   (D) Gateway

23. A communication device that combines transmissions from several I/O devices into one line is a
   (A) Concentrator
   (B) Modifier
   (C) Multiplexer
   (D) Full duplex file

24. Which layers of the OSI determines the interface often system with the user?
   (A) Network
   (B) Application
   (C) Data link
   (D) Session

25. Which of the following of the TCP/IP protocols is used for transferring files from one machine to another?
   (A) FTP   (B) SMTP
   (C) SNMP   (D) RPE

26. In which OSI layers does the FDDI protocol operate?
   (A) Physical
   (B) Data link
   (C) Network
   (D) Both (A) and (B)

27. In FDDI, data normally travel on
   (A) The primary ring
   (B) The Secondary ring
   (C) Both rings
   (D) Neither ring

28. The _______ layer of OSI model can use the trailer of the frame for error detection.
   (A) Physical
   (B) Data link
   (C) Transport
   (D) Presentation

29. In a _______ topology, if there are n devices in a network, each device has n-1 ports for cables.
   (A) Mesh
   (B) Star
   (C) Bus
   (D) Ring

30. Another name for Usenet is
   (A) Gopher
   (B) Newsgroups
   (C) Browser
   (D) CERN

HOTS (ACHIEVERS SECTION)

31. Application layer (layer 4) in TCP/IP model corresponds to:
   (A) Layer 4 and 5 in OSI model
   (B) Layer 5 and 6 in OSI model
   (C) Layer 6 and 7 in OSI model
   (D) Layer 1 and 2 in OSI model

32. Which layers of the OSI model are host-to-host layers?
   (A) Transport, Session, Presentation, Application
   (B) Network, Transport, Session, Presentation
   (C) Datalink, Network, Transport, Session
   (D) Physical, Datalink, Network, Transport

33. What is the use of a router in a network?
   (A) Forwards a packet to all outgoing links
   (B) Forwards a packet to the next free outgoing link
   (C) Determines on which outing link a packet is to be forwarded
   (D) Forwards a packet to all outgoing links except the originated link

34. What is the use of Subnetting?
    (A) It divides one large network into several smaller ones
    (B) It divides network into network classes
    (C) It speeds up the speed of network
    (D) None of these

35. Which of the following is true about the Ping command?
    (A) Ping stands for Packet Internet Generator.
    (B) The ping command checks the port level connectivity between source destinations end points.
    (C) Ping summarizes the packet loss and round-trip delay between two IP end points.
    (D) The ping command activates the RARP protocol of the IP layer.

1.	Ⓐ Ⓑ Ⓒ Ⓓ	8.	Ⓐ Ⓑ Ⓒ Ⓓ	15.	Ⓐ Ⓑ Ⓒ Ⓓ	22	Ⓐ Ⓑ Ⓒ Ⓓ	29.	Ⓐ Ⓑ Ⓒ Ⓓ
2.	Ⓐ Ⓑ Ⓒ Ⓓ	9.	Ⓐ Ⓑ Ⓒ Ⓓ	16.	Ⓐ Ⓑ Ⓒ Ⓓ	23.	Ⓐ Ⓑ Ⓒ Ⓓ	30.	Ⓐ Ⓑ Ⓒ Ⓓ
3.	Ⓐ Ⓑ Ⓒ Ⓓ	10.	Ⓐ Ⓑ Ⓒ Ⓓ	17.	Ⓐ Ⓑ Ⓒ Ⓓ	24.	Ⓐ Ⓑ Ⓒ Ⓓ	31.	Ⓐ Ⓑ Ⓒ Ⓓ
4.	Ⓐ Ⓑ Ⓒ Ⓓ	11.	Ⓐ Ⓑ Ⓒ Ⓓ	18.	Ⓐ Ⓑ Ⓒ Ⓓ	25.	Ⓐ Ⓑ Ⓒ Ⓓ	32.	Ⓐ Ⓑ Ⓒ Ⓓ
5.	Ⓐ Ⓑ Ⓒ Ⓓ	12.	Ⓐ Ⓑ Ⓒ Ⓓ	19.	Ⓐ Ⓑ Ⓒ Ⓓ	26.	Ⓐ Ⓑ Ⓒ Ⓓ	33.	Ⓐ Ⓑ Ⓒ Ⓓ
6.	Ⓐ Ⓑ Ⓒ Ⓓ	13.	Ⓐ Ⓑ Ⓒ Ⓓ	20.	Ⓐ Ⓑ Ⓒ Ⓓ	27.	Ⓐ Ⓑ Ⓒ Ⓓ	34.	Ⓐ Ⓑ Ⓒ Ⓓ
7.	Ⓐ Ⓑ Ⓒ Ⓓ	14.	Ⓐ Ⓑ Ⓒ Ⓓ	21.	Ⓐ Ⓑ Ⓒ Ⓓ	28.	Ⓐ Ⓑ Ⓒ Ⓓ	35.	Ⓐ Ⓑ Ⓒ Ⓓ

PROGRAMMING IN SCRATCH 

LEARNING OBJECTIVES

➤ Basic Concepts of Scratch programming
➤ Different Panes in Scratch
➤ Different Blocks in Scratch

MULTIPLE CHOICE QUESTIONS

1. Scratch 3.0 was officially released in ______
   (A) 2010   (B) 2013
   (C) 2019   (D) None of these

2. ______ contains the set of blocks, which is used to program the sprite.
   (A) Blocks Palette   (B) Stage
   (C) Scripts Area   (D) None of these

3. ______ block draws a line as the sprite moves on the stage.
   (A) Pen down   (B) move 10 steps
   (C) turn 15 degrees   (D) None of these

4. Who is the founder of Scratch?
   (A) James Gosling   (B) Tim-Berners-Lee
   (C) Mitchel Resnick   (D) None of these

5. Blocks Palette is the place where you create a script for the Sprite to do a specific task.
   (A) True   (B) False

6. A script consists of at least two blocks.
   (A) True   (B) False

7. You can run the sprite only in clock-wise direction.
   (A) True   (B) False

8. Scratch 2.0 projects are saved with the extension .sb2.
   (A) True   (B) False

9. In scratch, a character or object is called?
   (A) Spirit   (B) Sprint
   (C) Sprite   (D) Split

10. What name is given to directive that tells the computer to do something?
    (A) Command   (B) Condition
    (C) Variable   (D) Event

11. Which expression is either true or false?
    (A) Numeric   (B) Algebraic
    (C) Boolean   (D) None of these

12. Blocks held inside which block loops till the condition is true?
    (A) If-then   (B) Repeat
    (C) Repeat until   (D) Forever

13. In Scratch, blocks whose label begin with broadcast signal ______.
    (A) Statement   (B) Condition
    (C) Variable   (D) Event

14. Performing an action depending on IF a criteria is met is called a
    (A) Sequence   (B) Statement
    (C) Loop   (D) Condition

15. The background of the stage can be changed using the instructions under the ______ block.
    (A) Looks   (B) Pen
    (C) Motion   (D) Events

16. Seven Lego BOOST stack blocks, _________ reporter blocks, ______ hat blocks, and ______ boolean block are included in Scratch 3.0.
    (A) Two, one, one
    (B) Two, two, one
    (C) Two, three, one
    (D) Two, three, two

17. Match them correctly:

S. No.	Blocks	S. No.	Scripts
1.	Events	A	turn clockwise 15 degrees
2.	Control	B	switch costume to costume2
3.	Sound	C	when flag clicked
4.	Motion	D	play sound 'meow' until done
5.	Looks	E	forever

    (A) 1- C; 2- E; 3 - D; 4 -A ; 5 - B;
    (B) 1- A; 2- E; 3 - D; 4 -C ; 5 - B;
    (C) 1- C; 2- E; 3 - D; 4 -B ; 5 - A;
    (D) 1- E; 2- C; 3 - A; 4 -D ; 5 - B;

18. Correct the order of the steps to delete an unwanted sprite from the stage

Step A — Select the sprite from the sprite list.

Step B — Click the 'Delete' button, available on the right top of the selected sprite.

Step C — The selected sprite will be deleted from the stage.
    (A) Step A, Step B, Step C
    (B) Step C, Step A, Step B
    (C) Step C, Step B, Step A
    (D) None of these

19. When you click the ________ tab, all backdrops you've loaded are listed in the panel to the left. To rename a backdrop, use the bar above the drawing area next to ________ to type a new name for the backdrop.
    (A) Backdrops, Costume
    (B) Costume, Backdrops
    (C) Factors, Costume
    (D) Backdrops, Factors

20. To select multiple objects, ______________ while selecting them.
    (A) click and drag, or hold Shift
    (B) double click Shift
    (C) double click Alt
    (D) press ALT + Shift

	A B C D		A B C D		A B C D		A B C D		A B C D
1.	Ⓐ Ⓑ Ⓒ Ⓓ	5.	Ⓐ Ⓑ Ⓒ Ⓓ	9.	Ⓐ Ⓑ Ⓒ Ⓓ	13	Ⓐ Ⓑ Ⓒ Ⓓ	17.	Ⓐ Ⓑ Ⓒ Ⓓ
2.	Ⓐ Ⓑ Ⓒ Ⓓ	6.	Ⓐ Ⓑ Ⓒ Ⓓ	10.	Ⓐ Ⓑ Ⓒ Ⓓ	14.	Ⓐ Ⓑ Ⓒ Ⓓ	18.	Ⓐ Ⓑ Ⓒ Ⓓ
3.	Ⓐ Ⓑ Ⓒ Ⓓ	7.	Ⓐ Ⓑ Ⓒ Ⓓ	11.	Ⓐ Ⓑ Ⓒ Ⓓ	15.	Ⓐ Ⓑ Ⓒ Ⓓ	19.	Ⓐ Ⓑ Ⓒ Ⓓ
4.	Ⓐ Ⓑ Ⓒ Ⓓ	8.	Ⓐ Ⓑ Ⓒ Ⓓ	12.	Ⓐ Ⓑ Ⓒ Ⓓ	16.	Ⓐ Ⓑ Ⓒ Ⓓ	20.	Ⓐ Ⓑ Ⓒ Ⓓ

INTRODUCTION TO PYTHON

LEARNING OBJECTIVES

- ➤ Introduction to Python
- ➤ Applications of Python
- ➤ Installation of Python
- ➤ Keywords, variables and data types in Python
- ➤ Different operators

MULTIPLE CHOICE QUESTIONS

1. Find the invalid variable among the following:
   - (A) 1st_string
   - (B) my_string_1
   - (C) _
   - (D) foo

2. The order of precedence in the Python language is:
   - A. Exponential
   - B. Parentheses
   - C. Division
   - D. Multiplication
   - E. Subtraction
   - F. Addition
   - (A) B,A,D,C,F,E
   - (B) A,B,D,C,F,E
   - (C) A,B,C,D,E,F
   - (D) B,A,D,C,E,F

3. Which one of these is incorrect?
   - (A) float('nan')
   - (B) float('inf')
   - (C) float('12+34')
   - (D) float('56'+'78')

4. The value of the Python expression given below would be:
   ```
   4+2**5//10
   ```
   - (A) 77
   - (B) 0
   - (C) 3
   - (D) 7

5. The return value for trunc() would be:
   - (A) bool
   - (B) float
   - (C) int
   - (D) None

6. The output of this Python code would be:
   ```
   s='{0}, {1}, and {2}'
   s.format('hi', 'great', 'day')
   ```
   - (A) 'hi, great, and day'
   - (B) 'hi great and day'
   - (C) 'hi, great, day'
   - (D) Error

7. The output of this Python code would be:
   ```
   a = ['mn', 'op']
   for i in a:
   i.upper()
   print(A)
   ```
   - (A) [None, None]
   - (B) ['MN', 'OP']
   - (C) ['mn', 'op']
   - (D) None of these

8. The output of this Python code would be:
   ```
   print("mno. PQR".capitalize())
   ```
   - (A) Mno. Pqr
   - (B) Mno. pqr
   - (C) MNO. PQR
   - (D) mno. pqr

9. Which arithmetic operators can we NOT use with strings?
   (A) –   (B) +
   (C) *   (D) All of these

10. Which function do we use to shuffle a list(say list1)?
   (A) shuffle(list1)
   (B) list1.shuffle()
   (C) random.shuffleList(list1)
   (D) random.shuffle(list1)

11. In the following statements of Python, which ones will result into the output: 6?
```
A = [[1, 2, 3],
[4, 5, 6],
[7, 8, 9]]
```
   (A) A[3][2]   (B) A[2][3]
   (C) A[1][2]   (D) A[2][1]

12. Is this code valid in Python?
```
>>> m=6,7,8,9
>>> m
```
   (A) No, many values will unpack
   (B) Yes, (6,7,8,9) will be printed
   (C) Yes, 6 will be printed
   (D) Yes, [6,7,8,9] will be printed

13. Which function removes a set's first and the last element from a list?
   (A) pop   (B) remove
   (C) dispose   (D) discard

14. The output of this Python code would be:
```
>>> x={1:"X",2:"Y",3:"Z"}
>>> del x
```
   (A) the del method does not exist for dictionary
   (B) the del would delete the values present in dictionary
   (C) the del would delete the entire dictionary
   (D) the del would delete all the keys in dictionary

15. The output of this Python code would be:
```
sum(1,2,3)
sum([2,4,6])
```
   (A) 6, 12   (B) Error, Error
   (C) Error, 12   (D) 6, Error

16. The output of this Python code would be:
```
def find(x, **y):
print(type(y))
find('letters',X='1',Y='2')
```
   (A) Dictionary
   (B) An exception is thrown
   (C) String
   (D) Tuple

17. Which one of these is NOT true about recursion?
   (A) We can replace a recursive function by a non-recursive function
   (B) The memory space taken by the recursive functions is more than that of non-recursive function
   (C) Running a recursive function is faster as compared to a non-recursive function
   (D) The process of recursion makes it easier for users to understand a program

18. The output of this Python code would be:
```
a = ['mn', 'op']
print(len(list(map(list, a)))))))
```
   (A) 4   (B) 2
   (C) Not specified (D) Error

19. Which of these functions can NOT be defined under the sys module?
   (A) sys.argv
   (B) sys.readline
   (C) sys.path
   (D) sys.platform

20. Which function doesn't accept any argument?
   (A) re.compile   (B) re.findall
   (C) re.match   (D) re.purge

21. What are the values of the following Python expressions?

    ```
    2**(3**2)
    (2**3)**2
    2**3**2
    ```

    (A) 512, 64, 512   (B) 512, 512, 512
    (C) 64, 512, 64   (D) 64, 64, 64

22. What will be the output of the following Python code?

    ```
    print("abc. DEF".capitalize())
    ```

    (A) Abc. def   (B) abc. def
    (C) Abc. Def   (D) ABC. DEF

23. Which of the following statements is used to create an empty set in Python?

    (A) ( )   (B) [ ]
    (C) { }   (D) set()

24. What will be the value of 'result' in following Python program?

    ```
    list1 = [1,2,3,4]
    list2 = [2,4,5,6]
    list3 = [2,6,7,8]
    result = list()
    result.extend(i for i in list1 if i not in (list2+list3) and i not in result)
    result.extend(i for i in list2 if i not in (list1+list3) and i not in result)
    result.extend(i for i in list3 if i not in (list1+list2) and i not in result)
    ```

    (A) [1, 3, 5, 7, 8]   (B) [1, 7, 8]
    (C) [1, 2, 4, 7, 8]   (D) error

25. What will be the output of the following Python program?

    ```
    def foo(x):
        x[0] = ['def']
        x[1] = ['abc']
        return id(x)
    q = ['abc', 'def']
    print(id(q) == foo(q))
    ```

    (A) Error   (B) None
    (C) False   (D) True

LATEST DEVELOPMENTS IN 'IT' 

LEARNING OBJECTIVES

➤ Latest developments in the field of IT

MULTIPLE CHOICE QUESTIONS

1. Which of the following features was introduced in iPhone 5S?
   - (A) IOS 7.0.6
   - (B) Wi-fi
   - (C) Touch ID
   - (D) Bluetooth 4.0

2. Storage in iPads is flash based because it is ______.
   - (A) Smaller size and faster start-up times
   - (B) Greater storage capacity
   - (C) Lower cost at the expanse of start-up speed
   - (D) All of these

3. An iPad smart cover saves energy. It does so because ______.

   - (A) It has a nub that hits the on-off switch.
   - (B) It covers the tablet's light sensor, causing it to go into the sleep mode.
   - (C) It does not affect the battery life. It's just there to protect the screen.
   - (D) All of these

4. SaaS stands for
   - (A) Software as a Service
   - (B) Similar assets as Service
   - (C) Software as a Security
   - (D) Security as a Service

5. When the twitter service is down, you would see ______ on the twitter site.
   - (A) Nothing
   - (B) A 404 file not found message
   - (C) The fail whale
   - (D) The twitter logo

6. Which of the following is not a category of cloud computing service?
   - (A) PaaS
   - (B) IaaS
   - (C) TaaS
   - (D) SaaS

7. Identify the following:

   It is a social networking website for people in professional occupations which was founded in December 2002 and launched on May 5, 2003. It is a mainly used for professional networking.
   - (A) Twitter
   - (B) Ibibo
   - (C) LinkedIn
   - (D) Facebook

8. A MacBook Air is just _______ thin.

(A) 1 Inch (2.5 cm)
(B) 2 Inches (5.1 cm)
(C) 3 Inches (7.6 cm)
(D) Less than 2 cm

9. It is a video game franchise created by Finnish computer game developer Rovio Entertainment. Inspired primarily by a sketch of stylized wingless birds, the first game was first released for Apple's IOS in December 2009.
(A) Farmville
(B) Angry birds
(C) StarWars
(D) Mafia Piggies

10. Which of the following sensors are present in Samsung Galaxy S5?
(A) Heart Rate
(B) Finger Sensor
(C) Gyro Sensor
(D) All of these

11. Double-click is a company. It produces cookies which _______.
(A) Contain a user's personal information
(B) Can track users across the Internet
(C) Are real fresh-baked cookies
(D) Can delete all cookies on your PC

12. Digital Fingerprinting is used for _______.
(A) Preventing users from uploading copyrighted videos
(B) Tracking peer-to-peer file sharing
(C) Preventing video duplication
(D) All of these

13. Which of the following Nintendo 3DS game was released on October 12, 2013?
(A) Mario Kart 7
(B) Pokemon X and Y
(C) Super Mario 3D land
(D) New Super Mario 3D Bros 2

14. How many transistors are included in the Intel Core i9 processor, introduced in 2023?
(A) 7 million
(B) 91 million
(C) 2.95 billion
(D) 4980 million

15. _______ is the extent to which a search engine indexes pages within a website.
(A) Crawl depth
(B) Search depth
(C) Crawl index
(D) Depth search

16. A wireless adapter for your PC or laptop plugs into all of the following except _______.
(A) PS2 port
(B) USB port
(C) PC card slot
(D) None of these

17. What is Google Keep?
(A) Google's new operating system for mobile devices.
(B) A digital scratchpad note taking application for the Android mobile OS.
(C) Google's new application for the cloud.
(D) Google's new web browser with advanced browsing features.

18. What is an Easter Egg?
(A) A secret message/view/screen in an application like MS-word typically used to display credits to the developments team.
(B) A secret message in some software which is displayed on the Easter eve
(C) A dangerous computer virus which was discovered on Easter
(D) A mobile operating system released on Easter, 2013

19. Web 3.0 is also called _______.
(A) The Semantic web
(B) The Interwebs
(C) Wimax
(D) All of these

20. The Mac Mini M2 runs on the _______ operating system.
(A) Mac OS
(B) Unix
(C) Windows
(D) Ubuntu

21. Which of the following is an online multiplayer gaming and digital media service for Xbox One?
    (A) Xbox Station
    (B) Xbox Live
    (C) Xbox Shipping
    (D) Xbox Digital

22. Convertible Laptops falls in the category of?
    (A) Hybrid Laptops
    (B) Analog Laptops
    (C) Stationary Laptops
    (D) Traditional Laptops

23. Collection of hardware devices installed in automobile to provide entertainment and information content are called?
    (A) Transport Embedded System
    (B) Planar Entertainment
    (C) Embedded Entertainment
    (D) In-Vehicle Infotainment

24. _______ is a toolkit marketed by its creators as an android remote administrative tool and it can be used to create "trojanized" apps?
    (A) Cendroid
    (B) Dendroid
    (C) Bendroid
    (D) Tentroid

25. Which of the following is NOT a type of display technology for Smartphone?
    (A) CRT
    (B) AMOLED
    (C) OLED
    (D) Retina Display

Darken Your Choice with HB Pencil

1. Ⓐ Ⓑ Ⓒ Ⓓ	6. Ⓐ Ⓑ Ⓒ Ⓓ	11. Ⓐ Ⓑ Ⓒ Ⓓ	16 Ⓐ Ⓑ Ⓒ Ⓓ	21. Ⓐ Ⓑ Ⓒ Ⓓ
2. Ⓐ Ⓑ Ⓒ Ⓓ	7. Ⓐ Ⓑ Ⓒ Ⓓ	12. Ⓐ Ⓑ Ⓒ Ⓓ	17. Ⓐ Ⓑ Ⓒ Ⓓ	22. Ⓐ Ⓑ Ⓒ Ⓓ
3. Ⓐ Ⓑ Ⓒ Ⓓ	8. Ⓐ Ⓑ Ⓒ Ⓓ	13. Ⓐ Ⓑ Ⓒ Ⓓ	18. Ⓐ Ⓑ Ⓒ Ⓓ	23. Ⓐ Ⓑ Ⓒ Ⓓ
4. Ⓐ Ⓑ Ⓒ Ⓓ	9. Ⓐ Ⓑ Ⓒ Ⓓ	14. Ⓐ Ⓑ Ⓒ Ⓓ	19. Ⓐ Ⓑ Ⓒ Ⓓ	24. Ⓐ Ⓑ Ⓒ Ⓓ
5. Ⓐ Ⓑ Ⓒ Ⓓ	10. Ⓐ Ⓑ Ⓒ Ⓓ	15. Ⓐ Ⓑ Ⓒ Ⓓ	20. Ⓐ Ⓑ Ⓒ Ⓓ	25. Ⓐ Ⓑ Ⓒ Ⓓ

LOGICAL REASONING

15

LEARNING OBJECTIVES

- Simple Analogy
- Classification
- Types of Series
- Concept of Finding Odd one out
- Single Alphabet and Alphabet group
- Concept of Coding and Decoding
- Number Test
- Time Sequence Test
- Concept of Alphabet Test
- Concept of Blood relation Test
- Concept of Mathematical Operations
- Types of Mathematical Operations
- Concept of Arithmetic Reasoning
- Types of Problems
- Concept of Inserting the missing character
- Problems based on continuation of figures
- Solving questions related to paper cutting
- Concept of Mirror Images
- Concept of Water Images

MULTIPLE CHOICE QUESTIONS

There is a certain relation between two given words on one side of : : and one word is given on another side of : : while another word is to be found from the given alternatives having the same relations with this word as the given pair has. Select the best alternative.

1. Misogamy : Marriage : : Misogyny : ?
   - (A) Husband
   - (B) Women
   - (C) Relations
   - (D) Children

2. Coherent : Consistent : : Irate : ?
   - (A) Unhappy
   - (B) Irritated
   - (C) Angry
   - (D) Unreasonable

3. Skirmish : War : : Disease : ?
   - (A) Patient
   - (B) Medicine
   - (C) Infection
   - (D) Epidemic

4. Accomodation : Rent : : Journey : ?
   - (A) Octroi
   - (B) Fare
   - (C) Freight
   - (D) Expense

5. Elegance : Vulgarity : : Graceful : ?
   - (A) Comely
   - (B) Awkward
   - (C) Dirty
   - (D) Asperity

Directions (6–10): Find the missing term(s).

6. 101, 100, ?, 87, 71, 46.
   - (A) 92
   - (B) 88
   - (C) 89
   - (D) 96

7. 100, 50, 52, 26, 28, ?, 16, 8.
   - (A) 30
   - (B) 36
   - (C) 14
   - (D) 32

8. 6, 24, 60, 120, 210, 336, ?, 720
   - (A) 496
   - (B) 502
   - (C) 504
   - (D) 498

9. 3, 1, 4, 5, 9, 14, 23, ?
   - (A) 32
   - (B) 37
   - (C) 41
   - (D) 28

10. 3, 6, 18, 72, 360, ?
    (A) 720   (B) 1080
    (C) 1600   (D) 2160

Find the odd one out:

11. 3, 5, 11, 14, 17, 21
    (A) 21   (B) 17
    (C) 14   (D) 3

12. 8, 27, 64, 100, 125, 216, 343
    (A) 27   (B) 100
    (C) 125   (D) 343

13. 10, 25, 45, 54, 60, 75, 80
    (A) 10   (B) 45
    (C) 54   (D) 75

14. 396, 462, 572, 427, 671, 264
    (A) 396   (B) 427
    (C) 671   (D) 264

15. 6, 9, 15, 21, 24, 28, 30
    (A) 28   (B) 21
    (C) 24   (D) 30

16. If TRAIN is coded as RPYGL, the code for SCOOTER would be
    (A) QAMMRCP   (B) QBNNRCP
    (C) QAMMSBP   (D) QBNNSBP

17. If SCIENCE is coded as UFJTJM, GENE will be coded as:
    (A) HGQI   (B) IHRJ
    (C) IHRI   (D) IHSJ

18. If EQOKYO stands for DOLLAR and QQXMBP stands for POUNDS, then MARKET stands for:
    (A) NYOLGW   (B) NYOGLW
    (C) LYOLGW   (D) NYOLWG

19. If in a certain code MANISH is written as NZMRHS, then how will RANJITA be written in the same code?
    (A) IZMQRGZ   (B) IZMPRGZ
    (C) IZMQRHZ   (D) IZMQRIZ

20. If GOOD is written HQRH, how will you write DREAM?
    (A) ESPBN   (B) ETHER
    (C) ETHPQ   (D) ESHDR

21. One evening before sunset, two friends Amit and Sunit were talking to each other face to face. If Sunil's shadow was exactly to his left side, which direction was Amit facing?
    (A) North
    (B) South
    (C) West
    (D) Inadequate data

22. A postman was returning to the post office, which was in front of him to the North. When the post office was 100 meters away from him, he turned to the left and moved 50 meters to deliver the last letter at Shanti villa. He then moved in the same direction for 40 meters, turned right and moved 100 meters further. How many meters was he away from the post office?
    (A) 0   (B) 90
    (C) 150   (D) 100

23. Two buses start from the opposite points of a main road, 150 kms apart. The first bus runs for 25 kms and takes a right turn and runs for another 15 kms. It then, turns left and runs for another 25 kms and takes the direction back to reach the main road. In the meantime, due to a minor breakdown, the other bus has run only 35 kms along the main road. What would be the distance between the two buses at this point?
    (A) 75 kms   (B) 870 kms
    (C) 65 kms   (D) 85 kms

24. A man is facing West. He turns 45 degrees in the clockwise direction and then another 180 degrees in the same direction and then 270 degrees in the anticlockwise direction. Which direction is he facing now?
    (A) South   (B) North-West
    (C) West   (D) South-West

25. A started walking from a place. After walking for a kilometer, he turned left and walked for a half km, he again turned left. Now, he is walking torwards east. In which direction, did he originally start?

(A) West   (B) East
(C) South   (D) North

26. Raju is 5th from the left and Pankaj is 12th from the right end in a row of students. If Pankaj shifts three places towards Raju, his position is 10th from the left. How many students are there in the row?

(A) 24   (B) 28
(C) 26   (D) 27

27. If the day after tomorrow is Saturday. What day was three days before yesterday?

(A) Monday   (B) Sunday
(C) Friday   (D) Tuesday

28. In a particular year 1st November is Wednesday what day was 1st October in that year?

(A) Tuesday   (B) Sunday
(C) Friday   (D) Monday

29. How many days will be there from 26th January 2008 to 15th may 2008 if both days included?

(A) 114   (B) 113
(C) 117   (D) 111

30. Some students stand in a row. Manish's position is 19th from both the ends. How many students are there in that row?

(A) 37   (B) 41
(C) 39   (D) 42

31. If the English alphabet is written in reverse order then what will be the 4th letter to the right of 13th letter from the left?

(A) G   (B) J
(C) L   (D) K

32. If in the English alphabet, starting from 5th letter from the left, if 12 letters are written in reverse order then which letter will be 7th to the left of 14th letter from the right?

(A) L   (B) O
(C) M   (D) N

33. If 1st and 26th, 2nd and 25th, 3rd and 24th and so on, letters of English alphabet are paired then when of the following pair is correct?

(A) CW   (B) IP
(C) GR   (D) EV

34. If the order of English alphabet is reversed which will be the 8th letter to the right of O?

(A) W   (B) V
(C) G   (D) E

35. In the given arrangement which letter is 10th to the right of the letter which is exactly the middle letter between F & D?

F J M P O W R N B E Y C K A V L D G X U H Q I S Z T

(A) X   (B) U
(C) H   (D) G

36. Pointing towards Meena, Rajan said, "I am the only son of her mother's son." How is Meena related to Rajan?

(A) Mother
(B) Aunt
(C) Niece
(D) Cousin

37. Introducing Rekha, Sarita said, "she is the only daughter of my father's only daughter." How is Sarita related to Rekha?

(A) Mother
(B) Niece
(C) Cousin
(D) Aunt

38. Pointing to Kanchan, Sulekha said, "He is the son of my father's only son." How is Kanchan's mother related to Sulekha?

(A) Sister

(B) Aunt

(C) Daughter

(D) Sister-in-law

39. Mohan told Rajesh, "Yesterday I defeated the only brother of the daughter of my grandmother." Whom did Mohan defeat?

(A) Son

(B) Brother

(C) Father

(D) Cousin

40. Pointing to a man in a photograph, a woman said, "His brother's father is the only son of my grandfather." How is the woman related to the man in the photograph?

(A) Sister

(B) Aunt

(C) Daughter

(D) Mother

Choose the code letters that you think describes the shape in the box on the right hand side and circle the letter on the answer sheet, or mark the appropriate box on the multiple choice answer sheet.

41. Which figure completes the series?

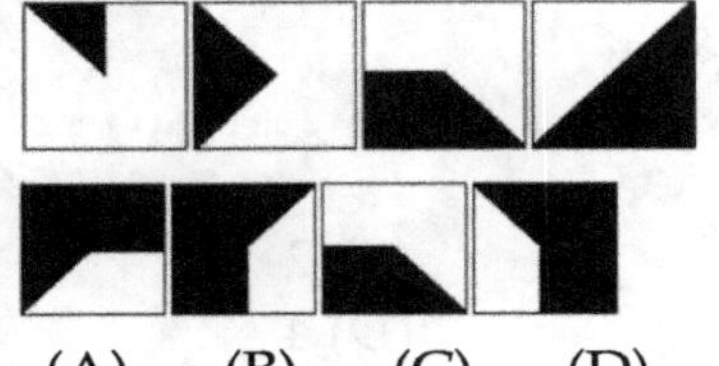

(A)   (B)   (C)   (D)

42. Which figure completes the series?

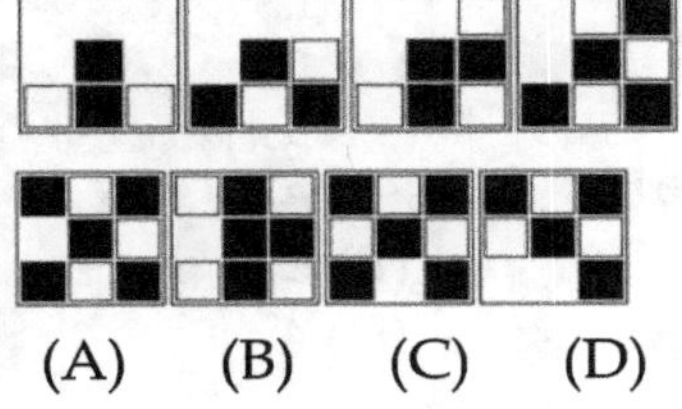

(A)   (B)   (C)   (D)

43. Which figure completes the series?

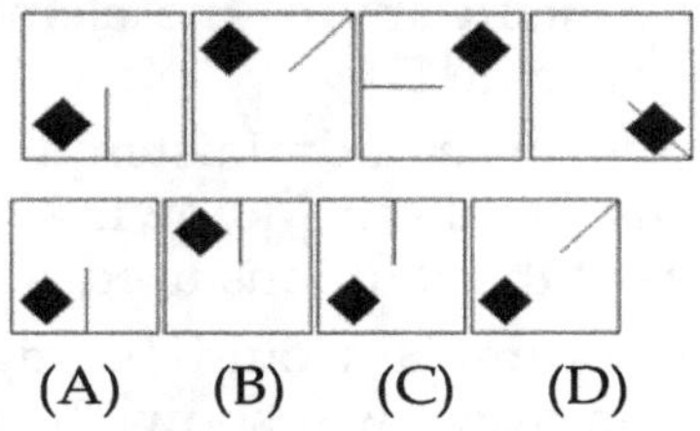

(A)   (B)   (C)   (D)

44. Which figure completes the series?

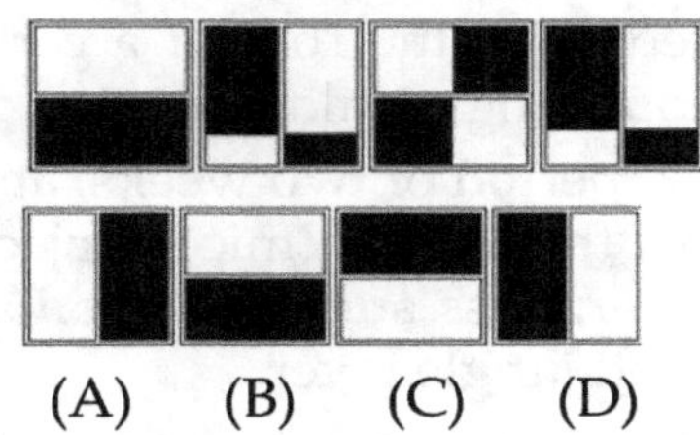

(A)   (B)   (C)   (D)

45. Which figure completes the series?

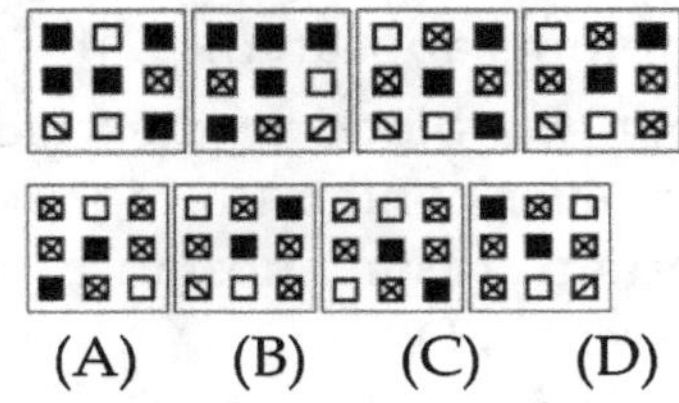

(A)   (B)   (C)   (D)

Direction (46–47): In an experiment conducted at a laboratory, 160 white mice were injected with Serum D. Another 160 white mice were injected with a harmless sugar solution. In two weeks time, 39% of the white mice, injected with Serum D contracted the highly contagious and often fatal disease 'jungle fever'. Hence, it can be concluded that 'jungle fever' is caused by some elements similar to the elements in Serum D.

46. The above discussion would be weakened most severely in case it is shown that:

(A) People contracting 'jungle fever' are usually the victims of the bite of the South American Lesser Hooded Viper.

(B) One among the 160 white mice had already contracted 'jungle fever' prior to the laboratory experiment.

(C) The natural habitats of white mice do not contain any of the elements found in Serum D.

(D) The scientists administered the injections without knowing the contents of the solutions used.

47. The above argument would be highly empowered in case it was shown that:

(A) Some of the elements in Serum D are extracted from the root of a certain poisonous jungle wild flower.

(B) Within a period of two weeks, about 40% of the white mice, injected with a harmless sugar solution also contracted jungle fever.

(C) Almost all the white mice died within a period of two days after the first symptoms appeared.

(D) Invariably' the blood of the victims of jungle fever contains a high level of a certain toxic substance also found in serum D.

48. Distribution of leaflets and delivering speeches on government property should be outlawed. Radicals and fanatics have no right to use public property when peddling their unsavoury views.

The argument above is based on the postulate:

(A) The general public has a special concern in the free exchange of different political views.

(B) Radicals and fanatics prefer the use of public property while propagating their viewpoint.

(C) Every person who hands out leaflets and delivers speeches is a radical or fanatic.

(D) Legal constraints which are applicable to one group need not be equally applicable to all.

Direction (49–50): Come back with us to the real America leaving behind the turmoil of civilization. The real America is still inhabited by the eagle, the buffalo, the mountain lion and elk; it is still spacious, sprawling and majestic. Experience the freedom and serenity still to be found in here.

49. Choose the best option to title the above statement:

(A) The natural beauty of our land
(B) The fascinating urban centres
(C) The wild terrain of Africa
(D) One's own subconscious

50. The above paragraph is most likely to appear in which of the following?

(A) A Hunter's Guide to The United States
(B) Exploring the Great Outdoors
(C) The Quiet Beauty of Alaska
(D) How the Eagle Became Extinct

51. Choose the alternative which closely resembles the mirror image of the given combination.

ANS43Q12

(The four options below are printed as mirror images.)

(1) ANS43Q12
(2) ANS43Q12
(3) ANS43Q12
(4) ANS43Q12

(A) 1   (B) 2
(C) 3   (D) 4

52. Choose the alternative which closely resembles the mirror image of the given combination.

TARAIN1014A

(The four options below are printed as mirror images.)

(1) TARAIN1014A
(2) TARAIN1014A
(3) TARAIN1014A
(4) TARAIN1014A

(A) 1   (B) 2
(C) 3   (D) 4

53. Choose the alternative which closely resembles the mirror image of the given combination.

1965 INDOPAK

(The four options below are printed as mirror images.)

(1) 1965 INDOPAK
(2) 1965 INDOPAK
(3) 1965 INDOPAK
(4) 1965 INDOPAK

(A) 1   (B) 2
(C) 3   (D) 4

54. Choose the alternative which closely resembles the mirror image of the given combination.

MALAYALAM

(1) MALAYALAM   (2) MAJAYAJAM

(3) MAᒐAYAᒐAW   (4) MAᒐAYAᒐAM

(A) 1   (B) 2

(C) 3   (D) 4

55. Choose the alternative which closely resembles the mirror image of the given combination.

EFFECTIVE

(1) ƎVITƆƎꟻꟻƎ   (2) EVITCEFFE

(3) ƎꟻꟻƎƆTIVƎ   (4) ƎVITƆƎꟻꟻƎ

(A) 1   (B) 2

(C) 3   (D) 4

——————— Darken Your Choice with HB Pencil ———————

1.	Ⓐ Ⓑ Ⓒ Ⓓ	12.	Ⓐ Ⓑ Ⓒ Ⓓ	23.	Ⓐ Ⓑ Ⓒ Ⓓ	34.	Ⓐ Ⓑ Ⓒ Ⓓ	45.	Ⓐ Ⓑ Ⓒ Ⓓ
2.	Ⓐ Ⓑ Ⓒ Ⓓ	13.	Ⓐ Ⓑ Ⓒ Ⓓ	24.	Ⓐ Ⓑ Ⓒ Ⓓ	35.	Ⓐ Ⓑ Ⓒ Ⓓ	46.	Ⓐ Ⓑ Ⓒ Ⓓ
3.	Ⓐ Ⓑ Ⓒ Ⓓ	14.	Ⓐ Ⓑ Ⓒ Ⓓ	25.	Ⓐ Ⓑ Ⓒ Ⓓ	36.	Ⓐ Ⓑ Ⓒ Ⓓ	47.	Ⓐ Ⓑ Ⓒ Ⓓ
4.	Ⓐ Ⓑ Ⓒ Ⓓ	15.	Ⓐ Ⓑ Ⓒ Ⓓ	26.	Ⓐ Ⓑ Ⓒ Ⓓ	37.	Ⓐ Ⓑ Ⓒ Ⓓ	48.	Ⓐ Ⓑ Ⓒ Ⓓ
5.	Ⓐ Ⓑ Ⓒ Ⓓ	16.	Ⓐ Ⓑ Ⓒ Ⓓ	27.	Ⓐ Ⓑ Ⓒ Ⓓ	38.	Ⓐ Ⓑ Ⓒ Ⓓ	49.	Ⓐ Ⓑ Ⓒ Ⓓ
6.	Ⓐ Ⓑ Ⓒ Ⓓ	17.	Ⓐ Ⓑ Ⓒ Ⓓ	28.	Ⓐ Ⓑ Ⓒ Ⓓ	39.	Ⓐ Ⓑ Ⓒ Ⓓ	50.	Ⓐ Ⓑ Ⓒ Ⓓ
7.	Ⓐ Ⓑ Ⓒ Ⓓ	18.	Ⓐ Ⓑ Ⓒ Ⓓ	29.	Ⓐ Ⓑ Ⓒ Ⓓ	40.	Ⓐ Ⓑ Ⓒ Ⓓ	51.	Ⓐ Ⓑ Ⓒ Ⓓ
8.	Ⓐ Ⓑ Ⓒ Ⓓ	19.	Ⓐ Ⓑ Ⓒ Ⓓ	30.	Ⓐ Ⓑ Ⓒ Ⓓ	41.	Ⓐ Ⓑ Ⓒ Ⓓ	52.	Ⓐ Ⓑ Ⓒ Ⓓ
9.	Ⓐ Ⓑ Ⓒ Ⓓ	20.	Ⓐ Ⓑ Ⓒ Ⓓ	31.	Ⓐ Ⓑ Ⓒ Ⓓ	42.	Ⓐ Ⓑ Ⓒ Ⓓ	53.	Ⓐ Ⓑ Ⓒ Ⓓ
10.	Ⓐ Ⓑ Ⓒ Ⓓ	21.	Ⓐ Ⓑ Ⓒ Ⓓ	32.	Ⓐ Ⓑ Ⓒ Ⓓ	43	Ⓐ Ⓑ Ⓒ Ⓓ	54.	Ⓐ Ⓑ Ⓒ Ⓓ
11.	Ⓐ Ⓑ Ⓒ Ⓓ	22.	Ⓐ Ⓑ Ⓒ Ⓓ	33.	Ⓐ Ⓑ Ⓒ Ⓓ	44.	Ⓐ Ⓑ Ⓒ Ⓓ	55.	Ⓐ Ⓑ Ⓒ Ⓓ

MODEL TEST PAPER

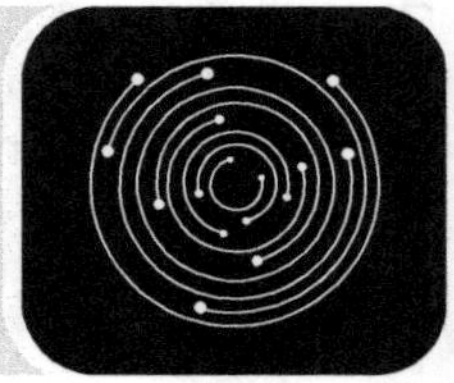

MULTIPLE CHOICE QUESTIONS

Logical Reasoning

1. In a game Kamini scored 199 and this raised her average over a number of games from 177 to 178. To raise her average to 179 with the next game she must score _______.
   (A) 179   (B) 180
   (C) 199   (D) 201

2. A bag contains 20 marbles coloured red, white, blue, green. There is one more red than white, 4 more white than blue and one more blue than green. The number of red marbles is _____.
   (A) 8   (B) 2
   (C) 7   (D) 10

3. There are two coins, one is double-headed and the other is normal. Shilpi tosses both coins. How many possible outcomes are there?
   (A) 2   (B) 1
   (C) 3   (D) 4

4. Prashant Jain has three children – Gauri, Vaibhav and Arun. Arun married Kanika, the eldest daughter of Mr. and Mrs. Mittal. The Mittal's married their youngest daughter to the eldest son of Mr. and Mrs. Sharma and they had two children named Akash and Shreya. The Mittal's have two more children, Shan and Rinki, both elder to Vanshika. Sameer and Ajay are sons of Arun and Kanika. Rashmi is the daughter of Akash. What is the surname of Rashmi _______ .
   (A) Sharma   (B) Mittal
   (C) Jain   (D) None of these

5. Six children B, D, C, M, J and K are split into two groups of three each and are made to stand in two rows in such a way that a child in one row is exactly facing a child in the other row. M is not at the ends of any row and is to the right of J, who is facing C. K is to the left of D, who is facing M. Which of the following groups of children is in the same row?
   (A) BDC   (B) BMD
   (C) MJK   (D) BMJ

6. Komal faces towards north. Turning to her right, she walks 25 metres. She then turns to her left and walks 30 metres. Next, she moves 25 metres to her right. She then turns to her right again and walks 55 metres. Finally, she turns to the right and moves 40 metres. In which direction is she now from her starting point?
   (A) South-west
   (B) South
   (C) North-west
   (D) South-east

7. In a row of girls, Rita and Monika occupy the ninth place from the right end and tenth place from the left end, respectively. If they interchange their places, then Rita and Monika occupy seventeenth place from the right and eighteenth place from the left respectively. How many girls are there in the row?
   (A) 25
   (B) 26
   (C) 27
   (D) Data inadequate

8. If 'X $ Y' means 'X is not greater than Y'; 'X % Y' means 'X is not smaller than Y'; 'X * Y' means 'X is neither smaller than nor equal to Y'; 'X @ Y' means 'X is neither greater than nor equal to Y'; then which of the following are the best conclusions for statements below?

Statements: D $ K, H * B, K @ H

Conclusions: I. B % K II. B @ K III. H * D

(A) Only I and II are true
(B) Either I or II is true
(C) Only I and III are true
(D) None of these

9. Following are the eligibility criteria for applying for the post of officer in a bank:

I. The candidate should be a graduate with at least 65 % marks.

II. The candidate should have at least 60% marks in graduation if he has post-graduate with at least 65% marks

III. The candidate should have at least 55% marks in graduation and at least 60% marks in postgraduation if he holds a doctoral degree (Ph.D.)

IV. The candidate should have at least 55% marks in both graduation and in post-graduation if he has at least five years work experience after post-graduation.

V. The candidate should have at least 60% marks in graduation if he has at least ten years work experience after graduation.

Mansi Roy has secured 65% marks in graduation and 50% marks in post-graduation. She has been working for ten years after completing her Ph.D. Which of the given above eligibility criteria is match with Mansi's eligibility for Bank.

(A) I only
(B) I and II only
(C) I and III only
(D) I and V only

10. A bowl of sweets was placed on a table to be distributed among three brothers – Rohan, Sahil and Keshav. Rohan arrived first and ate what he thought was his share of sweets and left. Then, Sahil arrived. He thought that he was the first one to arrive and ate the number of sweets, he thought was his share and left. Lastly, Keshav arrived. He again thought he was the first one to arrive and he took what he thought was his share. If 16 sweets are left in the bowl finally, how many sweets did the bowl contain initially?

(A) 27   (B) 36
(C) 48   (D) 54

11. If the number of students in 2004–2005 is increasing by 9.09% over the previous year, then total number of MBA students in the session of 2004–05 is ______.

(A) 555   (B) 600
(C) 777   (D) None of these

12. ______ are assumptions which are obvious universal truths.

(A) Theorem   (B) Axioms
(C) Statements   (D) Remark

13. If the code of 'ALTERED' is 'ZOGVIVW', what is the code of 'RELATED'?

(A) IVOZGVW   (B) IVOZGWV
(C) IVOGZVW   (D) VIOZGVW

14. Question given below is based on the following information:

(i) Six flats on a floor in two rows facing North and South are allotted to P, Q, R, S, T and U.

(ii) Q gets a North facing flat and is not next to S.

(iii) S and U get diagonally opposite flats.

(iv) R next to U, gets a South facing flat and T gets a North facing flat.

Which of the following combinations get South facing flats?

(A) QTS

(B) UPT

(C) URP

(D) Data is inadequate

15. If P + Q means P is the brother of Q; P ×
    Q means P is the father of Q and P – Q
    means P is the sister of Q, which of the
    following relations shows that I is the
    niece of K?

    (A) K + Y + Z – I

    (B) K + Y × I – Z

    (C) Z – I × Y + K

    (D) K × Y + I – Z

Computers and Information Technology

16. Which of the following types of RAM
    modules would you prefer to buy if you
    own a notebook computer or a small
    computer which has limited space?

    (A) SO-DIMM

    (B) RIMM

    (C) SIMM

    (D) SIPP

17. ALU is the part of a

    (A) CPU

    (B) Hardware

    (C) Software

    (D) Antivirus

18. Magnetic tape reader is a

    (A) Memory storage device

    (B) Input device

    (C) Output device

    (D) Processing device

19. GPU stands for

    (A) Graphics Processing Unit

    (B) Geographic processing unit

    (C) Graphics processor unit

    (D) Graphical Processing Unit

20. CU is the

    (A) Central unit

    (B) Control Unit

    (C) Circle unit

    (D) Combination Unit

21. Scripts are commonly used when
    designing a webpage. What are scripts?

    (A) A library of HTML pages

    (B) An executable file which contains a
        list of functions

    (C) A list of variables defined and used
        in HTML page

    (D) A list of executable commands to
        provide additional functionality on
        a Web page

22. Raster graphic is made of

    (A) Colours   (B) Pixels

    (C) Dots   (D) Rectangles

23. This is one of the topology.

    (A) Animal topology

    (B) Plant topology

    (C) Tree topology

    (D) Human topology

24. What happens if we press Shift+s in MS
    Word.

    (A) The letter S is typed in capital letter

    (B) The entire text gets selected

    (C) The programs saves the file

    (D) The program closes the file

25. The three buttons at the top right corner
    of the MS Word window are

    (A) Close, Exit and Stop

    (B) Minimize, Maximize and Close

    (C) Restore, Maximize and Close

    (D) Minimize, Maximize and Restore

26. What does a keyboard have?

    (A) Keys   (B) Buttons

    (C) Rolling balls   (D) Scroll wheel

27. Some mouse activities are

    (A) Click

    (B) Double click

    (C) Right click

    (D) All of these

28. The blinking line on the MS Word Screen is called
    (A) Indicator   (B) Blinker
    (C) Cursor   (D) Starter

29. This generation of computers were huge and slow.
    (A) First generation
    (B) Third generation
    (C) Second generation
    (D) Fifth generation

30. This computer has the characters of both the analog and digital computers.
    (A) Analog computer
    (B) Hybrid computer
    (C) Super computer
    (D) Digital computer

31. Your personal computer is a type of
    (A) Minicomputer
    (B) Mainframe computer
    (C) Supercomputer
    (D) Micro computer

32. JAVA is a
    (A) Programming language
    (B) Virus
    (C) Hardware
    (D) Operating system

33. OCR is a/an
    (A) Output device
    (B) Input device
    (C) Processing device
    (D) Operating system

34. 1 KB is equal to
    (A) 1024 MB   (B) 1024 GB
    (C) 1024 KB   (D) 1024 TB

35. You have to insert a smiley image – smiley.gif in a HTML page that you are creating. You also want the smiley to be moving – changing from a laughing smiley to a crying smiley and so on. Assuming that the gif file has the necessary content to allow movement of images, which of the following HTML code will help you achieve the movement?
    (A) <img src="smiley.gif" alt="Smiley face" width="32" height="32">
    (B) <movingimg src="smiley.gif" alt="Smiley face" width="32" height="32">
    (C) <src="smiley.gif" alt="Smiley face" width="32" height="32" move ="YES">
    (D) <src="smiley.gif" alt="Smiley face" width="32" height="32" move ="LAUGH">
        <src="smiley.gif" alt="Smiley face" width="32" height="32" move ="CRY">

36. It is similar to a CPU.
    (A) CU   (B) ALU
    (C) GPU   (D) All of these

37. This computer uses binary units.
    (A) Analog computer
    (B) Digital computer
    (C) Hybrid computer
    (D) None of these

38. VAX36 is an example of a
    (A) Micro computer
    (B) Mainframe computer
    (C) Minicomputer
    (D) Supercomputer

39. Which of the following fonts is an example of a Serif typeface?
    (A) Courier New
    (B) Algerian
    (C) Verdana
    (D) Lucida Handwriting

40. This page layout software is the first choice for the newspaper and magazine publishers because of its large size. Which is it?
    (A) Corel Ventura
    (B) Adobe PageMaker
    (C) QuarkXpress
    (D) MS Publisher

41. These screens display 80 characters of data lines horizontally and 25 lines vertically.

(A) Printer   (B) Monitor
(C) Scanner   (D) Web cam

42. It is known as backup memory.
    (A) Secondary memory
    (B) Primary memory
    (C) RAM
    (D) ROM

43. Translators include
    (A) Interpreters
    (B) Compilers
    (C) Assemblers
    (D) All of these

44. The shortcut for cut and paste is
    (A) Ctrl + X and Ctrl + V
    (B) Ctrl + V
    (C) Ctrl + C
    (D) Ctrl + X

45. Floppy disc is a
    (A) Primary memory device
    (B) Secondary memory device
    (C) Main memory device
    (D) Volatile memory.

Achievers Section

46. Routing means the process of
    (A) Selecting the slowest path in a network
    (B) Selecting the fastest path in a network
    (C) Selecting the best path in a network
    (D) Selecting the least used path in a network

47. Which is the smallest network that can be formed?
    (A) LAN   (B) PAN
    (C) WAN   (D) MAN

48. What happens when you press Ctrl +H in MS Word?
    (A) The word is saved
    (B) The word is searched
    (C) The word is replaced
    (D) The word is erased

49. What happens when you press Ctrl + S in MS Word?
    (A) The file is saved
    (B) Th file is opened
    (C) The file is deleted
    (D) The file is copied

50. What is the easiest way to close the program?
    (A) Alt + F4
    (B) Click on the close button at the top right corner of the window
    (C) Right click and click on close
    (D) Shut down the computer

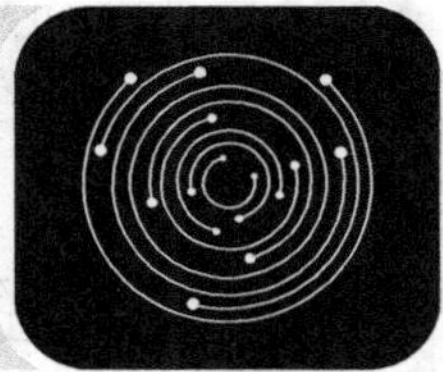

1. FUNDAMENTALS OF COMPUTER

Answer Key

1. (A)	2. (A)	3. (C)	4. (C)	5. (A)	6. (C)	7. (B)	8. (A)	9. (A)	10. (B)
11. (A)	12. (A)	13. (D)	14. (C)	15. (B)	16. (D)	17. (A)	18. (C)	19. (B)	20. (A)
21. (A)	22. (B)	23. (B)	24. (B)	25.(B)	26. (A)	27. (A)	28. (A)	29. (A)	30. (D)

HOTS (ACHIEVERS SECTION)

31. (C)	32. (D)	33. (D)	34. (D)	35. (A)

2. ALGORITHMS AND FLOWCHARTS

Answer Key

1. (C)	2. (A)	3. (C)	4. (A)	5. (C)	6. (C)	7. (D)	8. (B)	9. (B)	10. (A)
11. (B)	12. (C)	13. (B)	14. (A)	15. (D)	16. (A)	17. (A)	18. (B)	19. (B)	20. (A)
21. (B)	22. (C)	23. (D)	24. (A)	25. (C)	26. (A)	27. (B)	28. (A)	29. (D)	30. (D)

HOTS (ACHIEVERS SECTION)

31. (A)	32. (D)	33. (A)	34. (A)	35. (C)

33. (A)
Once a flowchart is drawn then it becomes cumbersome to modify it later.

35. (C)
In flowcharts each symbol has specific meaning and context in which they can be used, so, we cannot use symbol of our choice, because then it would become difficult for other users to understand the context in which you have used symbols.

3. ANIMATIONS AND MULTIMEDIA

Answer Key

1. (B)	2. (B)	3. (A)	4. (B)	5. (A)	6. (A)	7. (B)	8. (A)	9. (C)	10. (A)
11. (B)	12. (D)	13. (C)	14. (A)	15. (D)	16. (C)	17. (C)	18. (A)	19. (A)	20. (C)

1. (B)

   A green screen effect is used to superimpose anything or anyone into c photo or video. To apply this effect the background is covered with green scene.

5. (A)

   In interactive media the user can control the interaction with media elements Similar while chatting, user can decide what to type, to whom it should be sent, etc.

7. (B)

   A zoomable user interface is an interface that lets the user scale the viewable area.

12. (D)

   In cycle animation a series of frames or illustrations is drawn in sequence, and then they loop to create an animation.

17. (C)

   Rich media includes advanced features like audio, video and animations that appeal users to interact with the content.

HOTS (ACHIEVERS SECTION)

21. (A)	22. (B)	23. (A)	24. (C)	25. (B)

21. (A)

   The multiplane camera is a motion-picture camera that was used in the traditional animation process that moves a number of pieces of artwork past the camera at various speeds and at various distances from one another.

22. (B)

   J. Stuart Blackton made the first animated film in 1906. Humorous Phases of Funny Faces was the first animation film.

23. (A)

   Humorous Phases of Funny Faces was the first animation film made by J. Stuart Blackton. He was using a blackboard as his workplace together with chalk and an eraser as his main tools.

24. (C)

   Stop motion animation is used to animate things that are smaller than life size. Willis Harold O'Brian pioneered motion picture special effects, which were perfected in stop motion.

25. (B)

   J. Stuart Blackton made the first animated film in 1906. The film was entitled Humorous Phases of Funny Faces, and with this, he became known as the father of animation.

Answer Key

1. (A)	2. (B)	3. (D)	4. (A)	5. (C)	6. (C)	7. (D)	8. (C)	9. (B)	10. (A)
11. (B)	12. (D)	13. (B)	14. (A)	15. (C)	16. (A)	17. (D)	18. (B)	19. (C)	20. (C)

11. (B)

Adobe flash is proprietary software. It is available free for trial but only for a short period of time. So, it cannot be considered as free software.

13. (B)

To publish a file in Flash, go to File tab and select Publish operation.

17. (D)

A motion tween can be eased in or eased out using the motion property inspector. Ease In: The motion begins slowly, before gaining speed as time progresses. Ease Out: The motion begins quickly, before losing speed as time progresses.

HOTS (ACHIEVERS SECTION)

21. (B)	22. (C)	23. (B)	24. (C)	25. (A)

21. (B)

Library is a repository of reusable graphics, animations, buttons, sounds, videos in a flash file.

5. VISUAL BASIC

Answer Key

1. (B)	2. (A)	3. (C)	4. (C)	5. (A)	6. (D)	7. (C)	8. (A)	9. (A)	10. (D)
11. (B)	12. (A)	13. (A)	14. (B)	15. (D)	16. (A)	17. (D)	18. (B)	19. (B)	20. (D)
21. (B)	22. (B)	23. (C)	24. (D)	25. (B)	26. (A)	27. (C)	28. (A)	29. (B)	30. (D)

HOTS (ACHIEVERS SECTION)

31. (B)	32. (A)	33. (B)	34. (C)	35. (C)

31. (B)

Mod operator returns the remainder after division, so, the given arithmetic expression would evaluate as 1+1-2 →0.

33. (B)

Replace function returns a string in which a specified substring has been replaced with another string. Syntax of this function is: Replace (string, find, replace[, start[, count[, compare]]]).

6. HTML AND CSS

Answer Key

1. (C)	2. (D)	3. (D)	4. (B)	5. (C)	6. (C)	7. (D)	8. (B)	9. (A)	10. (A)
11. (A)	12. (D)	13. (C)	14. (C)	15. (C)	16. (D)	17. (D)	18. (A)	19. (A)	20. (D)

HOTS (ACHIEVERS SECTION)

21. (C)	22. (C)	23. (C)	24. (B)	25. (A)

23. (C)
<li> tag is used for displaying an unordered list using bullets, when <ul> or <ol> tag is not used.

25. (A)
The syntax of img tag is: <img src="url" alt="text"> Here url specifies the path where image is stored, and alt specifies the alternate text for the image.

7. MS WORD

Answer Key

1. (C)	2. (A)	3. (B)	4. (B)	5. (C)	6. (C)	7. (D)	8. (D)	9. (C)	10. (D)
11. (B)	12. (A)	13. (C)	14. (B)	15. (B)	16. (C)	17. (C)	18. (B)	19. (B)	20. (C)
21. (C)	22. (B)	23. (D)	24. (D)	25. (C)	26. (A)	27. (B)	28. (D)	29. (B)	30. (B)

HOTS (ACHIEVERS SECTION)

31. (A)	32. (C)	33. (C)	34. (D)	35. (C)

33. (C)
Word's Auto Recover feature saves information after specified minutes. You can change the time interval by going to Word Options → Save → change the time in "Save AutoRecover information after every" field.

35. (C)
Insert and link option insert the image in the word document and link it to the source file.

Answer Key

1. (B)	2. (B)	3. (C)	4. (B)	5. (B)	6. (D)	7. (A)	8. (D)	9. (C)	10. (B)
11. (D)	12. (D)	13. (A)	14. (C)	15. (D)	16. (C)	17. (A)	18. (C)	19. (B)	20. (A)
21. (D)	22. (B)	23. (C)	24. (B)	25. (D)	26. (D)	27. (D)	28. (A)	29. (C)	30. (A)

HOTS (ACHIEVERS SECTION)

31. (A)	32. (C)	33. (C)	34. (B)	35. (B)

31. (A)
Absolute reference is used to keep a row and/or column constant, because they do not change when copied or filled.

34. (B)
To display a message when unwanted data is entered in a cell, select the range of cells, then go to Data Validation option, select Error Alert tab and type error message and click on OK button.

9. MS POWERPOINT

Answer Key

1. (D)	2. (A)	3. (C)	4. (A)	5. (B)	6. (B)	7. (C)	8. (D)	9. (A)	10. (D)
11. (D)	12. (A)	13. (D)	14. (C)	15. (C)	16. (D)	17. (C)	18. (B)	19. (D)	20. (D)
21. (C)	22. (C)	23. (A)	24. (C)	25. (C)	26. (D)	27. (C)	28. (C)	29. (B)	30. (C)

HOTS (ACHIEVERS SECTION)

31. (C)	32. (C)	33. (D)	34. (A)	35. (B)

33. (D)
AutoFit Text to Placeholder option is available in AutoFit option, that gets displayed when a large block of text is inserted.

10. INTERNET AND VIRUSES

Answer Key

1. (D)	2. (C)	3. (B)	4. (A)	5. (D)	6. (C)	7. (A)	8. (C)	9. (A)	10. (D)
11. (C)	12. (D)	13. (B)	14. (C)	15. (C)	16. (B)	17. (B)	18. (A)	19. (B)	20. (A)
21. (D)	22. (C)	23. (B)	24. (D)	25. (D)					

1. **(D)**

The internet is a global network formed by connecting wide area networks (WANs), enabling worldwide communication and data sharing.

2. **(C)**

The ISPs (Internet Service Providers) are the main agents through which every computer is connected to the internet. They are licensed to allot public IP addresses to its customers in order to connect them to the internet.

3. **(B)**

DSL (Digital Subscriber Line) is the technology designed to use the existing telephone lines to transport high-bandwidth data to service subscribers. DSL was used to allow the early users access to the internet and it provides dedicated, point-to-point, public network access.

4. **(A)**

ISPs exchange internet traffic between their networks by using Internet Exchange Points. ISPs and CDNs are connected to each other at these physical locations are they help them provide better service to their customers.

5. **(D)**

HTTP is used to browse all the websites on the World Wide Web, DHCP is used to allot IPs automatically to the users on the internet, and DNS is used to connect the users to the host servers on the internet based on the Domain Name.

6. **(C)**

An IPv6 address is 128 bits long. Therefore, 2128 i.e. 340 undecillion addresses are possible in IPv6. IPv4 has only 4 billion possible addresses and IPv6 would be a brilliant alternative in case IPv4 runs out of possible new addresses.

7. **(A)**

Packet switching is the method based on which the internet works. Packet switching features delivery of packets of data between devices over a shared network.

8. **(C)**

Resource reservation protocol is a transport layer protocol used on the internet. It operates over IPv4 and IPv6 and is designed to reserve resources required by the network layer protocols.

9. **(A)**

DHCP stands for Domain Host Control Protocol. It is responsible to remotely assign IP address to the clients connected to the internet. The server that performs this fuction is called the DHCP server.

10. **(D)**

Packet switching is not really related to media access control as it just features delivery of packets of data between devices over a shared network. Internet is actually based on packet switching.

11. **(C)**

There are a total of 10 types of virus. These are categorized based on their working and characteristics. These are System or Boot Sector Virus, Direct Action Virus, Resident Virus, Multipartite Virus, Polymorphic Virus, Overwrite Virus, Space-filler Virus, File infectors, Macro Virus, Rootkit virus.

12. **(D)**

Types of viruses are System or Boot Sector Virus, Direct Action Virus, Resident Virus, Multipartite Virus, Polymorphic Virus, Overwrite Virus, Space-filler Virus, File infectors, Macro Virus, Rootkit virus. Trojan does not come under types of virus.

13. (B)

A computer virus is a malicious code which self-replicates by copying itself to other programs. The computer virus gets spread by itself into other executable code or documents. The intention of creating a virus is to infect vulnerable systems.

14. (C)

The ideal means of spreading computer virus are through emails, USB drives that are used portable and injected and ejected in different systems as well as from infected websites. Antivirus selling vendors do not place a virus in their CDs and DVDs.

15. (C)

In mid-1981, the 1st virus for Apple computers with the name Apple II came into existence. It was also called Elk Cloner, which resided in the boot sectors of a 3.3 floppy disk.

16. (B)

In mid-1981, the 1st virus for Apple computers with the name Apple II came into existence. It was also called Elk Cloner, which resided in the boot sectors of a 3.3 floppy disk.

17. (B)

The virus hides itself from getting detected in three different ways. These are by encrypting itself, by altering the disk directory with additional virus bytes or it uses stealth algorithm to redirect disk data.

18. (A)

Boot Sector Virus infects the master boot record & it is a challenging & a complex task to remove such virus. Mostly such virus spreads through removable devices.

19. (B)

Direct Action Virus gets installed & stays hidden in your computer's memory. Such type of virus stays involved to the specific type of files which it infects.

20. (A)

Direct Action Virus is also known as a non-resident virus which gets installed & stays hidden in your computer's memory. Such type of virus stays involved to the specific type of files which it infects.

21. (D)

Multipartite Virus infects the executables as well as the boot sectors. It infects the computer or get into any system through multiple mediums and are hard to remove.

22. (C)

Polymorphic Virus is difficult to identify as they keep on changing their type and signature. They're not easily detectable by traditional antivirus. It usually changes the signature pattern whenever it replicates itself.

23. (B)

Overwrite virus deletes all files that it infects. It can be removed by only deleting those infected files. Mostly, it gets spread via emails.

24. (D)

Space-fillers are a special type of virus which usually does not cause any serious harm to the system except it fills up the empty space in memory and codes leading to wastage of memory.

25. (D)

Computer virus is not created for protection. Virus writers may have other reasons like for research purpose, pranks, vandalism, financial gain, identity theft, and some other malicious purposes.

26. (D)	27. (C)	28. (B)	29. (D)	30. (D)

26. (D)

Multipartite Virus infects the executables as well as the boot sectors. It infects the computer or get into any system through multiple mediums and are hard to remove.

27. (C)

Explanation: Polymorphic Virus is difficult to identify as they keep on changing their type and signature. They're not easily detectable by traditional antivirus. It usually changes the signature pattern whenever it replicates itself.

28. (B)

Overwrite virus deletes all files that it infects. It can be removed by only deleting those infected files. Mostly, it gets spread via emails.

29. (D)

Space-fillers are a special type of virus which usually does not cause any serious harm to the system except it fills up the empty space in memory and codes leading to wastage of memory.

30. (D)

Computer virus is not created for protection. Virus writers may have other reasons like for research purpose, pranks, vandalism, financial gain, identity theft, and some other malicious purposes.

11. COMMUNICATION TECHNOLOGY

Answer Key

1. (A)	2. (C)	3. (A)	4. (C)	5. (C)	6. (A)	7. (C)	8. (B)	9. (A)	10. (A)
11. (D)	12. (C)	13. (A)	14. (C)	15. (B)	16. (A)	17. (A)	18. (A)	19. (C)	20. (D)
21. (B)	22. (D)	23. (C)	24. (B)	25. (A)	26. (D)	27. (A)	28. (B)	29. (A)	30. (B)

HOTS (ACHIEVERS SECTION)

31. (C)	32. (A)	33. (C)	34. (A)	35. (C)

12. PROGRAMMING IN SCRATCH

Answer Key

1. (C)	2. (A)	3. (A)	4. (C)	5. (B)	6. (A)	7. (B)	8. (A)	9. (C)	10. (A)
11. (C)	12. (C)	13. (D)	14. (D)	15. (A)					

13. INTRODUCTION TO PYTHON

Answer Key

1. (A)	2. (A)	3. (C)	4. (D)	5. (C)	6. (A)	7. (C)	8. (B)	9. (A)	10. (D)
11. (C)	12. (B)	13. (A)	14. (D)	15. (C)	16. (A)	17. (C)	18. (D)	19. (B)	20. (D)

HOTS (ACHIEVERS SECTION)

21. (A)	22. (A)	23. (D)	24. (A)	25. (D)

21. (A)

Expression 1 is evaluated as: 2**9, which is equal to 512. Expression 2 is evaluated as 8**2, which is equal to 64. The last expression is evaluated as 2**(3**2). This is because the associativity of ** operator is from right to left. Hence the result of the third expression is 512.

22. (A)

The first letter of the string is converted to uppercase and the others are converted to lowercase.

23. (D)

{ } creates a dictionary not a set. Only set() creates an empty set.

24. (A)

Here, 'result' is a list which is extending three times. When first time 'extend' function is called for 'result', the inner code generates a generator object, which is further used in 'extend' function. This generator object contains the values which are in 'list1' only (not in 'list2' and 'list3').

Same is happening in second and third call of 'extend' function in these generator object contains values only in 'list2' and 'list3' respectively.

So, 'result' variable will contain elements which are only in one list (not more than 1 list).

25. (D)

The same object is modified in the function.

14. LATEST DEVELOPMENTS IN 'IT'

Answer Key

1. (C)	2. (A)	3. (B)	4. (A)	5. (C)	6. (C)	7. (C)	8. (D)	9. (B)	10. (D)
11. (B)	12. (A)	13. (B)	14. (C)	15. (A)	16. (A)	17. (B)	18. (A)	19. (A)	20. (A)

21. (B)	22. (A)	23. (D)	24. (B)	25. (A)

15. LOGICAL REASONING

Answer Key

1. (B)	2. (C)	3. (D)	4. (B)	5. (B)	6. (D)	7. (C)	8. (C)	9. (B)	10. (D)
11. (C)	12. (B)	13. (C)	14. (B)	15. (A)	16. (A)	17. (B)	18. (C)	19. (A)	20. (B)
21. (A)	22. (B)	23. (C)	24. (D)	25. (A)	26. (A)	27. (B)	28. (B)	29. (D)	30. (A)
31. (B)	32. (B)	33. (D)	34. (C)	35. (A)	36. (B)	37. (A)	38. (D)	39. (C)	40. (A)
41. (D)	42. (B)	43. (C)	44. (C)	45. (A)	46. (B)	47. (D)	48. (C)	49. (A)	50. (D)
51. (B)	52. (D)	53. (D)	54. (B)	55. (A)					

1. (B)
   First word is hatred for the second word.

2. (C)
   The word in each pair are synonyms of each other.

3. (D)
   The second word is more intense form of first word.

4. (B)
   Money paid for accommodation is called rent. Money paid for travel is called fare.

5. (B)
   The word in each pair are antonyms of each other.

26. (A)
   When Pankaj shifts 3 places towards Raju his position is 15th from right and 10th from left.
   $\therefore$ No. of students = 15 + 10 − 1 = 24 students.

27. (B)
   Day after tomorrow is Saturday, means today is Thursday. Yesterday was Wednesday, three days before Wednesday was Sunday.

28. (B)
   1st November is Wednesday.
   31st October is Tuesday.
   29th, 22th, 15th, 8th, 1st October was Sunday.

29. (D)
   January 2008 = 6 days
   February 2008 = 29 days
   March 2008 = 31 days
   April 2008 = 30 days
   May 2008 = 15 days
   Total number of days from 26th January 2008 to 15th May 2008
   = 6 + 29 + 31 + 30 + 15
   = 111 days

30. (A)
   Manish's position is 19th from both the ends.
   Total no. of students = 19 + 19 − 1 = 38 − 1 = 37

31. (B)
   As per question

   Z Y X W V U T S R Q P O N M L K J I H G F E D C B A
   13th   4th

   $\therefore$ J is required letter.

32. (B)

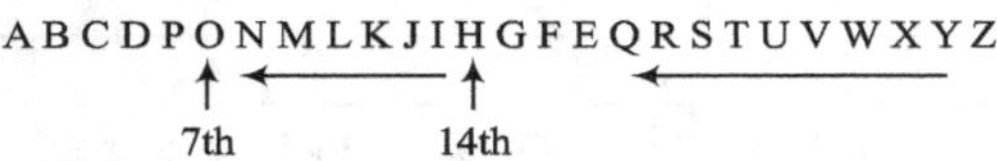

33 (D)

According to the question AZ, BY, CX, DW, EV, FU, GT, HS, IR, JQ, KP, LO, MN.

34. (C)

According to the question

ZYXWVUTSRQPONMLKJIHGFEDCBA

8th

36. (B)

Meena's mother's son = Meena's brother
Rajan is son of Meena's brother.
So, Meena is Rajan's aunt.

37. (A)

Sarita's father's only daughter means Sarita.
Rekha is Sarita's daughter.

38. (D)

Sulekha's fahter's only son = Sulekha's brother.
Kanchan is son of Sulekha's brother.
Kanchan's mother is wife of Sulekha's brother
So, Kanchan's mother is Sulekha's sister in law.

39. (C)

Daughter of grandmother = Aunt
Aunt's only brother = father

40. (A)

Only son of woman's grand father = woman's father
Man's brother's father = Man's father.

MODEL TEST PAPER

Answer Key

1. (D)	2. (A)	3. (A)	4. (A)	5. (D)	6. (D)	7. (B)	8. (D)	9. (D)	10. (D)
11. (B)	12. (B)	13. (A)	14. (D)	15. (B)	16. (A)	17. (A)	18. (B)	19. (A)	20. (B)
21. (D)	22. (B)	23. (C)	24. (A)	25. (B)	26. (A)	27. (D)	28. (C)	29. (A)	30. (B)
31. (D)	32. (A)	33. (B)	34. (D)	35. (A)	36. (A)	37. (B)	38. (C)	39. (B)	40. (C)
41. (B)	42. (A)	43. (D)	44. (A)	45. (B)	46. (B)	47. (B)	48. (C)	49. (A)	50. (A)

SAMPLE OMR ANSWER SHEET

1. STUDENT NAME (IN ENGLISH CAPITAL LETTERS ONLY)

Students must write and darken the respective circles completely using HB Pencil only. Othewise their Answer Sheets will not be evaluated.

PERSONAL DETAILS

2. SCHOOL CODE

3. CLASS

4. SECTION

5. ROLL NO.

6. QUESTION PAPER SET

A ○ B ○ C ○ D ○

7. MOBILE NUMBER

8. GENDER

MALE ○

FEMALE ○

9. STREAM
(Only for Class XI and XII Students)

MATHEMATICS ○
BIOLOGY ○
OTHERS ○

MARK YOUR ANSWERS

1.	Ⓐ Ⓑ Ⓒ Ⓓ	26.	Ⓐ Ⓑ Ⓒ Ⓓ
2.	Ⓐ Ⓑ Ⓒ Ⓓ	27.	Ⓐ Ⓑ Ⓒ Ⓓ
3.	Ⓐ Ⓑ Ⓒ Ⓓ	28.	Ⓐ Ⓑ Ⓒ Ⓓ
4.	Ⓐ Ⓑ Ⓒ Ⓓ	29.	Ⓐ Ⓑ Ⓒ Ⓓ
5.	Ⓐ Ⓑ Ⓒ Ⓓ	30.	Ⓐ Ⓑ Ⓒ Ⓓ
6.	Ⓐ Ⓑ Ⓒ Ⓓ	31.	Ⓐ Ⓑ Ⓒ Ⓓ
7.	Ⓐ Ⓑ Ⓒ Ⓓ	32.	Ⓐ Ⓑ Ⓒ Ⓓ
8.	Ⓐ Ⓑ Ⓒ Ⓓ	33.	Ⓐ Ⓑ Ⓒ Ⓓ
9.	Ⓐ Ⓑ Ⓒ Ⓓ	34.	Ⓐ Ⓑ Ⓒ Ⓓ
10.	Ⓐ Ⓑ Ⓒ Ⓓ	35.	Ⓐ Ⓑ Ⓒ Ⓓ
11.	Ⓐ Ⓑ Ⓒ Ⓓ	36.	Ⓐ Ⓑ Ⓒ Ⓓ
12.	Ⓐ Ⓑ Ⓒ Ⓓ	37.	Ⓐ Ⓑ Ⓒ Ⓓ
13.	Ⓐ Ⓑ Ⓒ Ⓓ	38.	Ⓐ Ⓑ Ⓒ Ⓓ
14.	Ⓐ Ⓑ Ⓒ Ⓓ	39.	Ⓐ Ⓑ Ⓒ Ⓓ
15.	Ⓐ Ⓑ Ⓒ Ⓓ	40.	Ⓐ Ⓑ Ⓒ Ⓓ
16.	Ⓐ Ⓑ Ⓒ Ⓓ	41.	Ⓐ Ⓑ Ⓒ Ⓓ
17.	Ⓐ Ⓑ Ⓒ Ⓓ	42.	Ⓐ Ⓑ Ⓒ Ⓓ
18.	Ⓐ Ⓑ Ⓒ Ⓓ	43.	Ⓐ Ⓑ Ⓒ Ⓓ
19.	Ⓐ Ⓑ Ⓒ Ⓓ	44.	Ⓐ Ⓑ Ⓒ Ⓓ
20.	Ⓐ Ⓑ Ⓒ Ⓓ	45.	Ⓐ Ⓑ Ⓒ Ⓓ
21.	Ⓐ Ⓑ Ⓒ Ⓓ	46.	Ⓐ Ⓑ Ⓒ Ⓓ
22.	Ⓐ Ⓑ Ⓒ Ⓓ	47.	Ⓐ Ⓑ Ⓒ Ⓓ
23.	Ⓐ Ⓑ Ⓒ Ⓓ	48.	Ⓐ Ⓑ Ⓒ Ⓓ
24.	Ⓐ Ⓑ Ⓒ Ⓓ	49.	Ⓐ Ⓑ Ⓒ Ⓓ
25.	Ⓐ Ⓑ Ⓒ Ⓓ	50.	Ⓐ Ⓑ Ⓒ Ⓓ

Signature of the Student & Date of Examination

Signature of the Invigilator & Date of Examination

V&S Publishers, F-2/16 Ansari Road, Daryaganj, New Delhi-110002, ☎ 011-23240026-27
✉ info@vspublishers.com, 🌐 www.vspublishers.com